GAUDETE

GAUDETE

by

Ted Hughes

HARPER & ROW, PUBLISHERS
New York, Hagerstown, San Francisco, London

FIRST U.S. EDITION

Library of Congress Cataloging in Publication Data

Hughes, Ted, 1930—
  Gaudete.
  I. Title.
PR6058.U37G3 1977   821'.9'14   77-3753
ISBN 0-06-012007-X

77 78 79 80 81 10 9 8 7 6 5 4 3 2 1

CONTENTS

If it were not Hades, the god of the dead and the underworld, for whom these obscene songs are sung and festivals are made, it would be a shocking thing, but Hades and Dionysos are one.

Heraclitus

Their battle had come to the point where I cannot refrain from speaking up. And I mourn for this, for they were the two sons of one man. One could say that 'they' were fighting in this way if one wished to speak of two. These two, however, were one, for 'my brother and I' is one body, like good man and good wife. Contending here from loyalty of heart, one flesh, one blood, was doing itself much harm.

PARZIVAL (Book XV)

ARGUMENT

An Anglican Clergyman, the Reverend Nicholas Lumb, is carried away into the other world by elemental spirits. Just as in the Folktale, these spirits want him for some work in their world.

To fill his place in this world, for the time of his absence, the spirits make an exact duplicate of him out of an oak log, and fill it with elemental spirit life. This new Nicholas Lumb is to all appearances exactly the same as the old, has the same knowledge and mannerisms, but he is a log. A changeling.

This changeling proceeds to interpret the job of ministering the Gospel of love in his own log-like way.

He organises the women of his parish into a coven, a love-society. And the purpose of this society, evidently, is the birth of a Messiah to be fathered by Lumb.

While he applies himself to this he begins to feel a nostalgia for independent, ordinary human life, free of his peculiar destiny.

At this point, the spirits who created him decide to cancel him. It may be that the original Lumb has done the work they wanted him to do, and so the changeling's time is up. The result is that all the husbands of the parish become aware of what is happening to their wives.

The narrative recounts the last day of the Changeling's life.

At the death of the changeling, the original Nicholas Lumb reappears in this world, in the West of Ireland, where he roams about composing hymns and psalms to a nameless female deity.

PROLOGUE

The Reverend Nicholas Lumb walks hurriedly over
cobbles through the oppressive twilight of an empty town,
in the North of England.

He has no idea where he is going. Or where he is.
Is it dusk or is it eclipse?
He urges himself, as if towards solid ground.
He concentrates on the jolt of his reaching stride and the
                         dragging flap of his cassock.

The sky is darkening.
The charred black chimneys jag up into the yellowish
                                               purple.
The stillness is every minute more awful
Like the dusk in a desert.

He walks with deliberate vigour, searching in himself for
                                control and decision.

He turns abruptly into a side-street
And is immediately stumbling.
He draws back to the wall.

All the length of the street, dead bodies are piled in heaps
       and strewn in tangles everywhere between the heaps.
Incredulous, he touches hands and faces.
He looks for wounds.
The jaws loll, as he lifts strengthless heads, which drop
                                back slack-necked.

Layered, interlocked, double-jointed, abandoned,
The corpses stare up into the purpled sky

Or at the black walls, or deeply into each other
As in the bottom of a mass-grave.

A mass-grave! The whole street is a mass-grave!

They were herded in here, then all killed together.
As they embraced each other, or fought to be free of each
                                  other, or clutched at each other.
Babies lie, tumbled separate, like refugee bundles.

   He turns again to find the empty street where he first
walked. But directions have shifted. And the street he
comes into is carpeted with corpses – the same. He clambers
over corpses, from street to street, turning and turning
among the streets, and every street is the same – a trench
of fresh corpses. Finally, he simply stands, listening to the
unnatural silence. He realises he is lost. The whole town is
a maze of mass-graves.

He begins to run.
He runs regardless of the soft hands, the spread hair.
As if he might outrun the swift developing cunning of this
                                                        maze,
Or the narrowing purpose of this twilight,
Or the multiplying corpses.

He begins to shout.
He shouts to strengthen his running.
And falls, and gets up from the dead, and shouts.

   And as he runs he hears another shout, in among his own
shouts. He stops and listens and shouts. And the shout
which answers is no echo. He shouts again, listening joy-
fully. At this moment he thinks only of another like him-
self, a lost man in the same plight, a comrade. And he hears
the shout searching through streets towards him. He runs,
shouting, to head it off, and to meet it.

12

And suddenly out of the twilight of corpses
A flapping shape –
A wild figure gyrating toward him.
A flailing-armed chimpanzee creature, bounding over the
                                         bodies and shouting.
Lumb has stopped.
This swirling apparition is something horrible.
A horrible revelation is hurtling towards him.
That shout is nothing but a mockery of his own shout.
The blackest clot of the whole nightmare has found a
                             shape and is leaping towards him.
Lumb's shout becomes a roar.

And the other stops, as if weightless.
A surprisingly small hunched figure.

Going forward Lumb finds an old man, in scarecrow rags,
gasping for breath – and laughing. Gasping not as if he had
exhausted himself with running, but as if he had laughed
himself helpless. Still gasping, and quaking with laughter,
he glances up at Lumb from tear-streaming eyes. A small
aged face, wild as a berry – the scorched, bristly, collapsed
face of a tinker.

Lumb stares down at him, too astonished to speak. He
waits for some explanation of the hilarity, and as if in
obedience the old man becomes solemn. He tells Lumb he
has been searching for him everywhere.

The voice is startling, abrupt, like a cattle-drover's. A
rough-snagged shillelagh of voice, hard and Irish. But
courteous, apologetic, almost affectionate. Lumb will have
to accompany him for some little distance.

But what about these corpses? What about these dead
people all over the town? What has happened? Lumb's
questions erupt. The old man turns away and starts
walking.

In a firelit, domed, subterranean darkness
Lumb stands, numbed

By a drum-beat, the magnification of heart-beat.
Who is the woman tangled in the skins of wolves, on the
                              rock floor, under the dome of rock?
And who is the aged aboriginal crouching beside her,
   stroking her brow, stroking the hair off her brow, with
   glistening fingers, with a trembling tenderness?
Shadows wrestle overhead in the dome gouged with
                                                    shadows.
Flames leap, glancing on the limbs of watchers under the
                                                      walls.
The firelight jerks in their eyes. Who are those watchers?

Lumb bends low
Over her face half-animal
And the half-closed animal eyes, clear-dark back to the
                                           first creature
And the animal mane
The animal cheekbone and jaw, in the fire's flicker
The animal tendon in the turned throat
The upper lip lifted, dark and clean as a dark flower
Who is this woman
And who is the ancient creature beside her?

Lumb kneels to understand what is happening
And what he is to do.
He thinks most likely this woman also is dead.

While the ancient man rocks back on his heels
And folds his long-boned hands over his skull
And mourns and cries.

Lumb feels for her absent pulse.
He lays his cheek to her lips
To feel her absent breath.
He lifts the moist eyelid open wider
And the startling brilliant gaze knifes into him
He stands in confusion
And looks round at the shadowed hollow faces

14

Crowding to enclose him
Eyepits and eyeglints

He declares he can do nothing
He protests there is nothing he can do
For this beautiful woman who seems to be alive and dead.
He is not a doctor. He can only pray.

He does not feel any blow. Only a sudden jagged darkness
that rends him apart, from the top of his skull downwards.
He sees lizard figures of lightning spurt up on all sides.
They pounce on him with pins and needles of claws. A
crushing weight rolls slowly across him. He understands it
is the bristling back of a gigantic man. He is able to inspect
minutely the leathery grain of the giant skin, a mosaic of
tiny lights like the eye of a fly, radiant as under a micro-
scope. He gazes into the widening beauty of this as the
weight of it descends and squashes him dark.

And now he feels grass under his hands. He opens his
eyes to a blue sky. Bright leaves hurt his head. He sits up
in the clearing of a steep, rocky wood. At first, in his daze,
it seems to him that lions lie all around him, watching him
lazily, but as they get to their feet he sees they are men.
He stands up with them, to be one of them, but their eyes
separate him from them. He is ordered to choose a tree. So
now, he thinks, they will hang me. And he looks at each
man in turn, intending to fix each face in his memory. But
even this exercise is frustrated. All these primitive, abor-
iginal faces around him are as alike as badgers.

He begins to speak. He would rather not choose a tree.
He would rather understand what is happening. He hears
his voice at a distance, as if he lay under anaesthetic. He
is aware that an arm has moved violently. A hard, heavy
whip, hard and heavy as a lump of wire cable, comes down
over the top of his bald skull. He sees every detail of the
pattern in the tight braid as a bright snake which bites
his lungs and flashes away downwards. He must choose a
tree.

He straightens from the pain and moves uphill and stops at the top, pointing to a young oak tree growing there on the summit between rocks. He considers taking his chance and bolting, but has already learned too well the reluctance of his limbs. At least he has picked a tree of distinction. But the next move surprises him, and without doubting for a moment that this is his own death in preparation, he becomes absorbed in watching.

Two men with axes fell the tree and trim the boughs, till the lopped trunk lies like a mutilated man, with two raised arms. Now Lumb is forced down, flat on his chest, and his arms are pulled above his head. Each of his wrists is tied to one of the two stumps. Because I am a priest, he is thinking, they will crucify me. The silent men arrange everything with great care. At last, Lumb and the tree lie, as if holding hands, their bodies stretched out opposite.

Now one of the men comes forward with a short heavy whip, and taking up his position starts to flog the senseless tree-bole. He swings the whip in a high arc, as if he intended each measured stroke to empty all his strength and be the last. As if he intended each stroke to cut the tree-bole through.

Lumb stares, uncomprehending, and tingling with the memory of that whip across his skull. Till a shock of real pain grips his back. His body clenches in spasm, like a fist. Hands lock round his ankles. Another whip is whistling in air, above him.

So, stroke by stroke, he and the tree-bole are flogged, tied together, until Lumb chews earth and loses consciousness.

He comes to, under heavy sloggings of cold water, naked and lying on concrete. Fingers unknot the cords which tie his wrists to the wrists of another man who sprawls, still unconscious, in torn and now sodden clerical garb. Through distorting water, Lumb sees this other is himself. He stares at him, in every familiar detail, as if he stared into the mirror. Seeing the ridged red track of the whipstroke across that glossy skull, Lumb feels gingerly over his own skull,

16

fingering for the corresponding welt or pain of it. He finds
only clean whole skin, without any tenderness. He reaches
to feel that lumped rawness on the skull of the other, but
hands jerk him upright, and turn him and hold him. And
so he stands, supported, on the wet concrete, under a high
steel roof.

A colossal white bull stands in front of him
Like the ceremonial image of god
That needs wheels. Its hooves splay
Under its ton and a half.
Ropes sag from its nose-ring
To either side, held by attendants.
Just as two others hold Lumb by the arms, facing the bull
Which now steps towards him
Deep-hulled, majestic, lifting each hoof as if from a great
                                                        depth
To join the momentum, getting its mountainous top-
                                        heavy sway moving
With gentle massaging tread,
Lifting its long piling power-wave towards him.
Lumb looks over the broad hump of neck
And down the long undulating range of its shoulders and
                                                        spine
Ugly with cobbled muscle, knotting and sliding
Under the silvered hide.
He sees its crooked knee-bosses calloused
By the kneeling weight of its own tonnage
As it halts, like a monument,
And sniffs ponderously towards his white naked feet
And the novel object of his streaming naked body
And, wakening a little, ponders him
With boyish, wicked, indifferent eyes.
Its head is like the capital
Of a temple column.
Then it forgets him, dozily masticating, happy behind the
                                        wall of its curls.
Lumb is handed a pistol.

17

A finger indicates with a tap the target-spot on the bull's
                                                    forehead.
Steadying the pistol
With both wet hands, which are shaking unrecognisably,
Lumb rests the muzzle in the white curls
Below the straight-out stumps of horns.

The bull gazes inward, nodding very slightly to
                            accommodate the work of its jaws,
Blinking sleepily, drooling a little,
And listening to the bull-music far back in the mountains
                                                    of its body.

And Lumb
Squeezes the pistol
Squeezing his eyes shut as the shot slams into his brain.

The bull's legs are in air.

Lumb huddles in a tight coil
On the puddled concrete, holding his splitting head
As if he had just dropped from a height.

Heavy cattle are surging through gangways
Driven through banging steel gates
By bellowing men
Who jab them with electrified clubs.
The white bull hangs from a winch
Like a cat swung up by the scruff of the neck.
Lumb is spreadeagled beneath it.
A long-handled hook rips the bull's underbelly from ribs
                                                    to testicles.
Half a ton of guts
Balloon out and drop on to Lumb.
He fights in the roping hot mass.
He pushes his head clear, trying to wipe his eyes clear.
Curtains of live blood cascade from the open bull above
                                                    him.

18

Wallowing in the greasy pulps, he tries to crawl clear,
But men in bloody capes are flinging buckets of fresh
blood over him.
Many bulls swing up, on screeching pulleys.
Intestines spill across blood-flooded concrete.
The din is shattering, despair of beasts
And roaring of men, and impact of steel gates.
Bull's skins stripped off, heads tumbling in gutters.
Carcases fall apart into two halves.

Lumb scrambles from the swamp.
He tries to wipe his eyes and to see.
Men crowd round him, laughing like madmen,
Emptying more buckets of the hot blood over him.
They are trying to drown him with blood
And to bury him in guts and lungs,
Roaring their laughter
As if they imitated lions.
Till he crawls on all fours to the wall, and hauls himself
up by the edge of a sliding steel door
And forces it open
As the men come at him, jabbing with their electrified
clubs
And roaring their infernal laughter
And he runs blind into pitch darkness and the din is
muffled away.

And he walks
With outstretched protecting arms
Till he sees a doorway to daylight.

He sees a ginnel, beyond it. Then stone steps upwards
into daylight. He stands at the bottom of the steps and
looks up at moving clouds. He hears street noises and sees
the top of a bus go past and a woman with shopping. A
mongrel dog peers down at him between rusty railings. He
turns back, and finds himself in a derelict basement full of
builder's old lumber. He looks down at his blood-varnished

19

body, crusting black, already flaking, and trembling with shock and bewilderment. He strives to remember what has just happened to him. He can no longer believe it, and concludes that he must have been involved in some frightful but ordinary accident. He searches round for some other exit from this basement, in growing agitation, but there is only the door to the street. He returns to the bottom of the steps and stands looking up again at the clouds, till his trembling becomes hard shivering. Suddenly he remembers the streets full of corpses, but his dread then was nothing like what he feels now. He forces himself to move.

He climbs the stone steps.

GAUDETE

Binoculars
Powerful, age-thickened hands.
Neglected, the morning's correspondence
Concerning the sperm of bulls.
The high-velocity rifles, in their glass-fronted cupboard,
Creatures in hibernation, an appetite
Not of this landscape.
Coffee on the desk, untasted, now cold,
Beside the tiger's skull – massive paperweight with a
    small man-made hole between the dragonish eye-
    sockets.

Major Hagen, motionless at his window,
As in a machan,
Shoulders hunched, at a still focus.

The parkland unrolls, lush with the full ripeness of the
last week in May, under the wet midmorning light. The
newly plumped grass shivers and flees. Giant wheels of
light ride into the chestnuts, and the poplars lift and pour
like the tails of horses. Distance blues beyond distance.

   The scene
balances on the worm's stealth, the milled focal adjustment,
under the ginger-haired, freckle-backed thick fingers and
the binocular pressure of Hagen's attention.
   Across the middle distance, beyond the wide scatter of
bulls, the prone stripe of the lake's length reflects the sky's
metals. Crawling with shadow, hackled with reeds, snaggy
with green bronze nymphs, maned with willows.

Everything hangs
In a chill dewdrop suspension,
Wobbled by the gossamer shimmer of the crosswind.

Hagen's face is graven, lichenous.
Outcrop of the masonry of his terrace.
Paradeground gravel in the folded gnarl of his jowls.

A perfunctory campaign leatheriness.
A frontal Viking weatherproof
Drained of the vanities, pickled in mess-alcohol and
                                            smoked dark.
Anaesthetised
For ultimate cancellations
By the scathing alums of King's regulations,
The petrifying nitrates of garrison caste.

A nerve is flickering
Under the exemplary scraped steel hair on the bleak
                                            skull,
But the artillery target-watching poise of his limbs,
                                stiff-kneed and feet apart,
Absorbs the tremor,

And the underlip, so coarsely wreathed
And undershot, like the rim of a crude archaic piece of
                                            earthenware

Is not moved
Forty generations from the freezing salt and the
                                            longships.

In his hardening lenses
The rhododendrons of the shrubbery island
Wince their chilled scarlet eruptions.

   The willows convulse, they coil and uncoil, silvery, like
swans trying to take off. Their long fringes keep lifting
from the Japanese bridge. On the bridge, two figures com-
plete the landscape artist's arrangement.

The Reverend Lumb's long sallow skull
Seeming dark as oiled walnut
Rests on the shoulder
Of Pauline Hagen, the Major's wife,
Whose body's thirty-five year old womb-fluttered
                                            abandon
Warms his calming hands
Beneath her ample stylish coat.

Her nerve-harrowed face
Crisping towards a sparse harvest handsomeness
Rests on his shoulder.
She has been weeping
And now looks through blur into the streaming leaf-shoal
                                            of the willows.

Lumb's downward gaze has anchored
On the tough-looking lilies, their clenched knob-flowers
In the cold morning water.
A deadlock of submarine difficulty
Which their draughty hasty lovemaking has failed to
                                            disentangle
And which has brought words to a stop.
Hagen
Contemplates their stillness. The man-shape
To which his wife clings.
He does not detect
Lumb's absence. He can watch his wife
But not the darkness into which she has squeezed her eyes,

The placeless, limitless warmth
She has fused herself into,
Clasping that shape
And shutting away the painful edges and clarities of the
                                        gusty distance,
Under the toppling continents of hard-blossomed cumulus
The tattery gaps of blue
And the high, taut mad cirrus.

The vista quivers.
Decorative and ordered, it tugs at a leash.
A purplish turbulence
Boils from the stirred chestnuts, and the spasms of the
                        new grass, and the dark nodes of bulls.

Hagen
Undergoes the smallness and fixity
Of tweed and shoes and distance. And the cruelty
Of the wet midmorning light. The perfection
Of the lens.
            And a tremor
Like a remote approaching express
In the roots of his teeth.

Hagen is striding
Exerting his leg-muscles, as if for health, breasting the
    oxygen, his cleated boots wrenching the gravel, down
    the long colonnade of chestnuts
Under the damp caves and black-beamed ruinous attics
Of intergroping boughs
That lean out and down over the meadow on either side,
Supporting their continents of leaf, their ramshackle
                        tottery masks.

His black labrador revolves passionately in its excite-
ments. His double-barrelled Purdey, cradled light in his
left elbow, feels like power. It feels like far-roaming tight-
ness, neatness, independence. With this weapon, Hagen is
happy. A lonely masterful elation bristles through him. He
glances constantly toward the perfection of the down-
sloping barrels, blue and piercing, snaking along beside him,
nosing over the poor grass and the ground ivy at the drive's
edge.

His features are fixed at enjoyment, a grille. He aims
himself, tight with force, down the tree-tunnel, at the cold
sheet of lakelight from which two figures, carefully separate,
are approaching.

A ringdove, tumbling with a clatter
Into wing-space
Under the boughs and between boles
And swerving up towards open field-light
Is enveloped by shock and numbness.
The bang jerks the heads of twenty bulls
And breaks up the distance.

A feather mop cavorts.

With a kind of gentleness
The Major's gingery horny fingers
Are gathering the muddled dove
From the labrador's black lips.

A wing peaks up at a wrong angle, a pink foot reaches
                                    deeply for safe earth.
Startlingly crimson and living
Blood hangs under his knuckles.
And the bird's head rides alert, as if on a tree-top,
A liquid-soft blue head floating erect, as the eye gimbals
And the Major presents it, an offering,
To his wife.
His machine laughter
Unconnected to any nerve
Is like the flame her face shrivels from.
Now he offers it to the priest
As the meaning of his grin, which is like the grin of a patient
After a mouth-operation.
Lumb's heavy hostile eye
Weighs what is ill-hidden.
The Major's carapaced fingers and his mask
Of military utility
Contort together, and the dove erupts underdown –
Tiny puffs and squirts.
He tosses it cartwheeling to Lumb
Who catches it
As if to save it, and clasps it to him
As if to protect it
Feeling its hard-core heat
And drinking its last cramping convulsions
Into the strength of his grip.
The Major calls his dog and stalks past these two, as on
                                    matters of higher command.
He leaves them
Under the breathing and trembling of the trees
Marooned
In the vacuum of his shot.

The dove's head, on its mauled neck,
Dangles like a fob,
Squandering its ruby unstoppably
Into the sterile gravel.

A mile away

Joe Garten, petty poacher and scrounger, in steep wood-
land, drives his narrow-bladed spade downward, deepening
his furrowed concentration. His bowed shoulders jerk
between the crumpled feet of gigantic beeches. His brow
shines and his yellow hair flings, in a slant mist of bluebells.
His moist eighteen year-old palms and fingers are jarred
hot and again jarred, against perverse roots and sudden
flints, as he follows his brown ferret cord down

Towards muffled subterranean
Thudding and squeals.

But now he comes weightlessly upright, hearing the wind-
carried bok of a twelve-bore.

He pinpoints it. He identifies it. He judges Hagen has
shot a woodpigeon on his morning walk. Every frond of the
wood listens with him.

His sweat glints, falling into the excavation. And as he
listens

A new presence, like a press of wind, fills up the air, a
thickening vibration. An echoing yawn of roar through
all the mass of leaves. It pours down the sunken road, ten
yards below him, among coiled, piling beech roots. And the
narrow, tree-choked valley is suddenly alert, alarmed, as
the sound ceases. Beside the little bridge in the bottom of
the wood, a white Ford Cortina has come to rest in the lay-
by.

Garten rises in his hole, peering. Mrs Westlake, the
doctor's wife, winds down her window, throws out a spent
match, puffs smoke, relaxes tensely, waits.

The wood creeps rustling back. The million whispering
busyness of the fronds, which seemed to have hesitated,
start up their stitchwork, with clicking of stems and all the
tiny excitements of their materials.

Garten half-lies, watching the white fox-fine profile,
under dark hair, in the car window. Her stillness holds him.

29

He eases his elbows and knees, hunching gently to his attentiveness, as to a rifle. His eyes, among bluebells and baby bracken, are circles of animal clarity, not yet come clear of their innocence.

Clouds slide off the sun. The trees stretch, stirring their tops. A thrush hones and brandishes its echoes down the long aisles, in the emerald light, as if it sang in an empty cathedral. Shrews storm through the undergrowth. Hover-flies move to centre, angle their whines, dazzle across the sunshafts. The humus lifts and sweats.

Garten's eyes are quiet, like a hunter's, watching the game feed closer. His heart deepens its beat, expectant.

His fantasy agitates, richly, monotonously, around the cool drawn features of Mrs Westlake, the high china cheek-bone, the dark mouth. A tentacle of her cigarette smoke touches his nostril, and hangs, in the lit woodland.

He fastens himself to her, as if to a magnification, fading from himself, like a motionless lizard.

One, two, three cigarettes. In the bird-ringing peace.

Pauline Hagen
Has turned back from the drive gate.
A leaf-bordered blankness
Like the suck of a precipice
Draws her along the bleak sweep of drive
Towards the white house.

Her legs move, as if to remain still were even more futile.
She looks upward
Into the open hanging underbellies of the trees
As if those puzzles held something from her.
As she walks
She feels too present, too tall, too vivid.

The level sprawl of world
Draws away tinily, in every direction.
It separates itself from her exposure.
She looks down
At the chaotic gravel.
Her eyes claw at the gravel.
Something in her is preparing a scream, which she dare
not utter.
Her legs carry her towards the house.
Twitchings jerk her eyelid, her cheek,
A tugging tightens her brow, so she has to rub her face in
her hands.

Something overpowering
Like an unmanageable horse, a sudden wild bulk
Starts rearing and wheeling away, to one side then to the
other
As if it would break out of her.
She halts, balancing giddily.
She has closed her eyes
Where Lumb is still with her
His presence strays all over her body, like a flame on oil,
His after-nearness, the after-caress of his voice
As if she breathed inside the silk of his nearness.

31

At the drive's edge, she kneels among bluebells.
She shuts her eyes more tightly.
The bunching beast-cry inside her shudders to be let out.
She folds her arms tightly
Over this rending,
She bends low, her face closes more tightly.
Her moan barely reaches the nearest tree.

She is gouging the leaf-mould,
She is anointing her face with it.
She wants to rub her whole body with it.
She is wringing the bunched stems of squeaking spermy
                                         bluebells
And anointing her face.
Lumb's glance keeps glimpsing through her body
Churning tracks of soft phosphorescence
Like the first sweaty wafts of a sickness.

She wants to press her face into the soil, into the moist
                                         mould,
And scream straight downward, into earth-stone darkness.
She cannot get far enough down, or near enough.

She hauls herself to her feet, towering
And walks
And enters the still house.

Rooms retreat.
A march of right angles. Barren perspectives
Cluttered with artefacts, in a cold shine.
Icebergs of taste, spacing and repose.

The rooms circle her slowly, like a malevolence.
She feels weirdly oppressed.
She remembers
A shadow-cleft redstone desert
At evening.
The carpet's edge. The parquet.

32

The door-knob's cut glass.
She observes these with new fear.
The kitchen's magenta tiles. The blue Aga.

It is her fifteen years of marriage
Watching her, strange-faced, like a jury.

Coffee from silver, to disarm some minutes.

Leaning against the bar of the stove
She meditates blankly,
Fixedly.
She is like the eye of a spirit level
Intent
On earth's poles, the sun's pull, the moon's imbalance.
A charioteer, for these moments,
On some rocking perimeter.

Major Hagen irrupts quietly into this sphere.
Controlling the explosive china with watchmender's touch,
                              he too drinks coffee.
He advances remotely, fumbling with keyhole words.
Suddenly he meets her small steady pupil
And sees her dry tangle of hair
And an outrage too dazzling to look at ignites the whole
                    tree of his nerves, a conflagration
Takes hold of everything –
His words seem to scald and corrupt his lips.
An insane voltage, a blue crackling entity
Is leaping around the kitchen
As if it had crashed in through the window.
Pauline Hagen feels her face go numb.
She stares at the black labrador
Which is enlarging, goggling, bristling
And snarling gape-mouthed.
Invisible hands
Are prising its jaws apart.

Hagen's face-crust has crimsoned. He is yelling.
An avalanche is on the move.
It will have to come.
There is so much he must not fail.
Humiliation of Empire, a heraldic obligation
Must have its far-booming say.
Three parts incomprehensible.
A frenzy of obsolete guns
Is banging itself to tatters
And an Abbey of Banners yells like an exhausted
                                    schoolmaster.
Arsenals of crazier energy open.
Depth charges
Of incredulity and righteousness
Search the taciturn walls and furniture.
Finally he just stands, gripping her shoulders,
Blasting her from all sides with voice.

She has shrivelled small, regaining her distance,
Trying to balance her coffee.

The labrador is spinning in a tight circle.
She sees the foam at its jaws.
And glances at Hagen – her half-anxiety
Outstripped by a quick smile, a flash of malice –
And the dog attacks him.

Its fangs hook in the weave of his jacket.
He flings it from him, barking its name, astonished.
It returns and clamps solidly on to the meat of his thigh.
He feels the shock of its hostility deeper than its fangs.
He kicks it away.
He bellows to overawe it.
It comes back
And leaps and leaps at his face.

Now Hagen
Swerves the full momentum of his rage on to the dog.
He lifts a chair.
This dog is going to account for everything.
Fangs splinter wood and wood shatters.
Only exhaustion will stop him.

Till at last he stands, trembling,
Like somebody pulled from an accident.
He drops the broken stump of his weapon.

He kneels
Beside the stilled heap of loyal pet
Hands huge with baffled gentleness
As if he had just failed to save it.
He lifts its slack head.
His horror is as dry
As volcanic rock.

His wife is watching him
As if it were all something behind the nearly unbreakable
                              screen glass of a television
With the sound turned off.

Lumb's voice
Is stroking her deeply,
Touching at her heart and lungs and bowels glancingly.
She goes on sipping her coffee.

Again
The tall woodland rains echo,
A descending hush of roar.
And the Minister's blue Austin van slides to a stop
Behind the white Ford.

Garten sinks to his knees
As if under the intensification of joy.
His lips
Surprisingly full red in the thin-skinned face
Filter crooked enlightenment.

The Reverend Lumb's long figure
Has emerged. Brisk
Under the muscled, sooted boles and silvery torsos of the
                                        uptwisting beeches
He appears tiny.
The long cassocked back
Is bending
At the Ford's suddenly open door.
He is leaning right inside.
Garten
Rises above the napes of tender curled bracken
As if clearing an aim

And he sees
The Minister's feet sprawling.
Lumb
Is fighting inside the car.
His hand
Claws for a grip on the car-top.
Suddenly he comes out backwards
As if tearing free
And the Ford roars out, its tyres rip dirt, it climbs
Away up through the tree tunnel of the opposite slope
In a burrowing fury.

Garten is erect, in open view, astounded – as if his
    rabbiting spade had spilled open a cache of ancient gold.

The Minister stands in the road
Mopping at his mouth. His white handkerchief
Brings away blood.
He and Garten inspect it thoughtfully
In the wood's
Torn, healing stillness.

Mrs Westlake

Arriving home, has left the car-door wide, and run
straight into the house, leaving that door wide too, right
back to the wall, as if she meant to snatch up just the few
essential things and leave this place forever –

She has already paused.
She stands
In the cool gleaming steel and copper stillness
Of her kitchen.
Stares at the bead on the cold water tap
Letting the scorchings sweep her throat and face.

She jerks back into control – hurries
From room to room, tense with purpose
Seeing nothing and arguing with everything.

All over her body the nerves of her skin smoulder.
The cream suit is an agony.
A lump of boiling electricity swells under her chest.
Wild cravings twist through her
To plunge to the floor
As if into a winter sea
And scour her whole body's length with writhings.
Sweat prickles her brow, she exclaims at the mirrors.

Her interrogation of Lumb is rearranging itself inside her.
A shifting of ponderous, underground machinery. A drag-
ging and swaying of unmanageable stage-partitions.

For long minutes, vacant,
She watches through a window, hardly breathing,
Mesmerised
By a distant conifer.

She is moving again, as if it were a last search for some-
thing hopelessly lost. Mirrors turn her back. A hateful
orange vase, a souvenir ashtray, present themselves briefly.

38

She finds herself now in one room, now in another, with a sensation of dropping through papery floors, falling from world to world.

As if hours had passed
She is sitting at a walnut veneer table.

She tilts her watch. As if in a doctor's waiting room. She has lit her last cigarette. Chill, comfortless, alien furniture. She is thinking: none of this has anything to do with me, and soon I shall be free.

She stares towards her husband's medical reference library, to numb herself on its dull morocco. It is no escape. Those volumes are swollen with the details of Lumb's body. Her brain swoons a little, trying to disengage. The glistening tissues, the sweating gasping life of division and multiplication, the shoving baby urgency of cells. All her pores want to weep. She is gripped by the weird pathos of bio-chemistry, the hot silken frailties, the giant, gristled power, the archaic sea-fruit inside her, which her girdle bites into, which begins to make her suit too tight.

She feels the finality of it all, and the nearness and greatness of death. Sea-burned, sandy cartilege, draughty stars, gull-cries from beyond the world's edge. She feels the moment of killing herself grow sweet and ripe, close and perfect.

The walls wait. The senseless picture frame.
Eyes half-closed
She sits stupidly, like something cancelled. Forcing the
seconds to pass.

Once, but more weakly and fleetingly than ever before, she imagines escaping to her sister in Reading. Her mother in Winchester. Rapidly she glances through the unbuttoning of coats, the worn-out exclamations, the glitter of curiosity, the celebration of tea and biscuits. Her drained,

39

cold fingers remain spread on the walnut veneer, above
their dim reflection. She stares into the fireplace.

She has already returned. She has already forgotten those
                                    afternoon ceilings
The cactus windowsills
The hall-chime nothingness.

   She is watching herself now, with richer satisfaction, in
Lumb's bedroom, tugging a knife through her throat. She
plans her splayed, last, carefully ghastly position.

Her mind closes.
Her stare comes to rest in the ashtray.
She can hear her watch whispering,
Listening to it, as if trapped inside it.
She has closed her eyes.

She waits
Like a beaten dog
At her trembling cigarette.

The scherzo
Of Beethoven's piano sonata Opus 109
Is devouring itself, dragonish,
Scattering scales,
Havocking polished, interior glooms,
Trembling dusty ivy, escaping towards the sky
Through the wedding of apple blossom at the open French
windows.

Jennifer is twenty two.
Under her loosened, jarred masses of chestnut
Her profile, long-nosed, lemuroid, lit,
Is pollen-delicate.
She is oppressed
By the fulness of her breasts, and the weight of flame in
her face.
She leans her trouble to the keyboard.

Observing her
Through the not-quite-closed corridor door
Her father listens, appalled.
The music flings in his face, it strikes at him
With derisive laughter and contemptuous shouts.
Her hands seem to be plunging and tossing inside his
chest.

His skull, glossy, veined, freckled, bulges
Over the small tight ferocious hawk's face
Evolved in Naval Command. Commander Estridge
Is stricken with the knowledge that his dream of beautiful
daughters
Has become a reality.
Simply, naturally, and now inevitably, there by the open
window.
The dream was as beautiful as the daughters.
But the reality
Is beyond him. Unmanageable and frightening.
Like leopard cubs suddenly full-grown, come into their
adult power and burdened with it.

41

Primaeval frames, charged with primaeval hungers and
                                    primaeval beauty.
Those uncontrollable eyes, and organs of horrific energy,
                                    demanding satisfaction.

The music she plays bewilders the old man.
He cannot interpret those atmospherics
And soundings and cries.
It is shouting something impossible, incomprehensible,
                                    monstrous.

The dutiful hands of his daughters
Which control his days
With routine breakfast egg and toast, with coffee,
With crisply ironed clothes, and warmed bed –
They are tearing him to pieces, elated
Under those sickly, sulphurous blooms
And the hellish upset of music.

In the dark hall, walled with stuffed wild life,
He listens. And he hears
Something final approaching.
Some truly gloomy horror is pushing.
Something that makes nothing of names, or affection, or
                                    loyalty, or consideration.
An evil
Like his own creeping, death-dawn-emptiness fear.
And he knows his daughters are in it, are part of it
Like the flames in fire.
He understands that it is so
And that there is now no other situation to manage but
                                    this
Which is beyond him
And that he can only wait for it, and that he is too old.
While the stuffed gulls around him vibrate,
And the stuffed falcons, the foxes, the stuffed great pike
With obedient eyes
And their panes vibrate.

42

The whole museum of dehydrated, memorial moults
Vibrates, helpless,
Under the girl's powerful, white, pouncing fingers.
Dwarfish and too old
He steps wirily down into the garden, under sagging
                                                    conifers
Which are still loaded with cavernous night-chill.
He spiders along the flagged moss-slimed path
And sees the big poppies, planted long ago by his wife,
Coming into bloom, and one, full out, has already dropped
                                    a crumpled blood-shard,
And he thinks yet again: Too late. And says aloud: I am
                                                    too late.
He is glad to be clear of his younger daughter
And of everything that pulses in her and swirls flaring
                                                    round her.
He climbs into the Belvedere at the end of the terrace
And closes the door
And sits. His bulging blood eyeball
Fixed in a lifetime of being imperious
Settles to the lens of the telescope.
He swings it on its pivot.

The village leaps towards him, opening its gardens and
                                                    doors.

But still the enraged
Albeit ephemeral music goes on
Like a materialised demon
Vandalising the ponderous ill-illumined Victorian house,
Beating at the faded ochre prints of imperial battles,
Re-animating
The arsenals of extinguished tribesmen
That trophy the walls.
It grips the cellars, feeling for the earth beneath
As if to lift the whole ungainly pile and shake off the
                                        chimneys.

It rushes up the servant's stair
With a fiery icy elation
Like the ghost of an imbecile calculator
Into the long attic.

The attic is an aviary.
Bleak prison boughs, polished by bird's feet, cage-wired
                                        windows.
Jays, magpies, crows, pigeons
Sitting in depressed jury.
Two macaws, seething their spite and lunacy.
Everywhere finches twitch and jitter.

Estridge's elder daughter, Janet,
Is examining her body,
Her swollen stomach, delicate glossed as the flank of a
                                        minnow,
In a long pierglass
Foxed with age, propped back among attic lumber,
Streaked with bird's droppings.

Her face, relaxed expressionless, as for a studio portrait,
Simply accepts the fate of being as it is.
She has made her decision
And is relieved not to be suffering any more.
No thought for the future falsifies these moments.
44

Her decision feels solid and good
Stronger than all the small appeals of tomorrow.
Like a final lying down into an immense weariness
It has relaxed her.

Now she can look at the birds,
Her father's prisoners,
Her girlhood's confidantes.
She sees just how squalid and miserable they are.
And they regard her too without any affection.

She rams out the frosted skylight with the back of a chair
And tells them to get back to their true friends
And true enemies.

She positions the chair.
She puts on her dressing gown, deliberately, feeling the
                              critical watchfulness of the birds.
She climbs onto the chair, balancing.
Arranges the hanging noose about her neck, lightly and
                                        attentively
As if she adjusted the collar of a dress.
Then tightens the knot, under the chin.
She ignores the tears
Which have come out on to her cheeks in fear and dismay.
She steps into space.

The birds
Alerted
By the waft of a strange predator, are suddenly smaller,
                                        tensed.

The chair topples, deciding a pigeon
To clap up through the window gap.
An opportunistic jay
Scrambles up the air and vanishes.
A magpie goes out like a bolt.

More and more rapidly follows the skulking departure of
                                                    the birds.
Only a crow, undecided, lingers.

While the music elbows nakedly in through the broken
    glass with the wet stirred freshness of the garden trees.

In Estridge's lens
A middle distance farm has come close.
Three fields beyond the farm, two men are cutting up a
blown-over beech-tree.
Holroyd employs one man.
Sitting under the farm's orchard wall, the minister's blue
Austin van,
Blossoms littering it.

Opening on to the closed yard, a barn-doorway, black.
Estridge is pleased with his telescope
Which brings him a hen flattened under a cock in the
barn doorway.
Then the birds scatter, long-legged.
Mrs Holroyd emerges, with dazzled eyes,
Carrying a basket, and adjusting her skirt,
And dusting herself down.
The Reverend Nicholas Lumb
Materialises out of the darkness behind her.
Mrs Holroyd, at twenty-seven, is a fresh-faced abundant
woman
With an easy laugh.
Estridge treasures her among his collection of ideals –
She reminds him of the country love of his youth, who
never appeared.

Now he watches Lumb
Following her closely to the house-door.
Within the hallway, within the magnified circle,
Turning, she sets Lumb's hands on her breasts and bites
his neck.

His hands gather up her skirts
As his foot closes the door
And Estridge's brain wrings
To a needling pang, as if a wire might snap.

His bulging eye
Hammers the blunt limits of objects and light.

Till a scream
Amplifies over his head's pain –
A repeated approaching scream, then a silence.
His younger daughter has left her piano.
She is running between the shrubs towards him.
He puts on his spectacles.
He quickly tries to think what could be the worst

                                                  possible.

He finds only helpless fear.
His daughter is screaming something at him
As if in perfect silence.

Lumb
Is looking at the land.
This is the unalterably strange earth.
He is looking at the sky. He looks down at the soil,
                                    between the grass.
He looks at the trees
Which clamber in a tangle up the slope towards him,
            from the river, out of the swell of land beyond.

He listens to all this, and listens into the emptiness beyond it
And the emptiness within it.
And the soft hollow air noises among it.

   It feels very like safety. If the trees were trees only, wood
only, were simple roots and boles and boughs and leaves,
and that only, as the stones should be stones. If the stones
were simple stones. This would be safe. All this would be
safety.

But he knows everything he looks at,
Even the substance of his fingers, and the near-wall of his
                                                        skin,
He knows it is vibrant with peril, like a blurred speed-
                                                vibration.
He knows the blood in his veins
Is like heated petrol, as if it were stirring closer and
                                    closer to explosion,
As if his whole body were a hot engine, growing hotter
Connected to the world, which is out of control,
And to the grass under his feet, the trees whose shadows
                                        reach for him.

He breathes deeply and strongly to confirm his solidity,
To cool his outline and his solidity
To fill his strength
Against the power that beats up against him, beating at
                            the soles of his feet,

49

Beating through his thoughts
And the obscure convulsions and blunderings of a music
                              that lurches through him
With brightenings and darkenings, and rendings and
                                             caressings,
With tiny crowded farness and near sudden hugeness
And hot twisting roughness, and vast cantileverings of
                                          star-balance.

He looks out across the quilt and embroidery of the
                                            landscape,
The hazings of distance, and the watery horizons folded
                                          like fingers,
And tries to imagine simple freedom –
His possible freedoms, his other lives, hypothetical and
                              foregone, his lost freedoms.
As each person carries the whole world, like a halo,
Albeit a dim and mostly provisional world, but with a
                         brightly focused centre, under the sun,
Considering their millions
All mutually exclusive, all conjunct and co-extensive,
He sees in among them,
In among all the tiny millions of worlds of this world
Millions of yet other, alternative worlds, uninhabited,
                                 unnoticed, still empty,
Each open at every point to every other and yet distinct,
Each waiting for him to escape into it, to explore it and
                                            possess it,
Each with a bed at the centre. A name. A pair of shoes.
                                       And a door.
And surrounded by still-empty, never-used limitless freedom.
He yields to his favourite meditation.
Forlorn, desperate meditation.

Between the root in immovable earth
And the coming and going leaf
Stands the tree
Of what he cannot alter.
50

As his heart surges after his reverie, with lofty cries and
                                    lifting wingbeats
Suddenly he comes against the old trees
And feels the branches in his throat, and the leaves at his
                                    lips.
He sees the grass
And feels the wind pulse over his skin.
He feels the hill he stands on, hunched, swelling,
Piling through him, complete and permanent with stone,
Filling his skull, squeezing his thoughts out from his eyes
To fritter away across surfaces.

Till the one presence of world crushes him from himself,
        and sits on him like an iron crown on a stone pillar,
Studded with baleful stones,
As if he were a child king, hoisted on to a granite throne,
                surrounded by eyes of sharpened metal.
For a half hour he stands, alert
Imprisoned in the globe's stoniness
And the thin skin, the thin painting of mother-soil,
And the hair-fine umbilicus of life in the stalk of grass.

His life returns as a fly. It lands on his eyelid and trickles
                down to his mouth-corner.
He moves to free himself.
Some animal is pushing noisily below in the wood.
A squirrel flees up through a beech, like a lashing rocket,
        and rips into the outermost leaf-net with a crash.
Voices recede, snatch back their words and meanings,
Become bramble stem, leaf hollows, reticulation of twigs.
He is clearly aware of himself, on the hill in clear light,
    from the eye of a soaring, reconnoitring and
    downsliding far crow.
He prays
To be guided. He feels his prayer claw at the air, as at
                                    glass
Like a beetle in a bottle.

He tries to pray with the sun –
Feeling it break off, dry in his mouth
He tries to find in himself the muscle-root of prayer.
He takes a few brisk steps
To tear free of his fear, to shake his limbs
Out of their crawling horror, their fly-tiny helplessness.

He makes an effort
To feel his plans steady. He fixes, hard and firm, phrasing
                                              it clearly,
His decision to escape before night.
This very day. To carry his body, with all its belongings,
Right to the end of its decision. Surely that is simple
                                                enough.
What is wrong with this idea? He only has to do it.
Surely it is all he wants to do.

He is afraid
As if he were asleep and dreaming the first warnings of
                                              smoke-smell
In a burning room, where everything is already
   spluttering and banging into flames, cores of fury
   drumming flames,
The flames swarming up, leaping like rats,
A torrent of devils twisting upwards above the tops of
                                            everything,
As if everything –
The whole world and day where he stands, trying to
                                            awake,
Were a giant aircraft out of control, shaking itself to
   pieces, already losing height, spinning slowly down in
   space
Scattering burning chunks,
The air sprayed with blazing fuel, full of an inaudible
                          screaming, sprayed with fine blood –

He leans his forehead to an ash tree, clasping his hands
                                      over his skull.

He presses his brow to the ridged bark.
He closes his eyes, searching.
He tries to make this ash-tree his prayer.
He searches upward and downward with his prayer,
 reaching upwards and downwards through the capillaries,
Groping to feel the sure return grasp
The sure embrace and return gaze of a listener –

He sinks his prayer into the strong tree and the tree
                              stands as his prayer.

The Bridge Inn bar
Is gleaming, the mopped floor drying
In the morning's leisured vacancy.
The door standing open, to ventilate last-night's beer-
                                                    smell,
Admits the conversation of the river and its stones.
The fleeing needle-cry of a dipper going downstream
Pierces the company of empty chairs.
Betty, the girl behind the bar,
Is making the last few preparations
For the first lunchtime regulars.
She is lean as a skinny boy and blonde as straw.
She takes a hot pie from the counter-oven
With pink bony hands
And goes back through the house.
The usual word to the pub-owner's wife, Mrs Walsall,
Who is peeling potatoes in the kitchen.
She is just slipping home with this lunch for her old mum
Before the first customers.
She cycles out of the yard, Mrs Walsall watches the
                                                    window.
Betty does not pass the window.
Mrs Walsall opens the latch and leans out. Betty
Is cycling along the lane beside the river, away from the
                                                    village.
Mrs Walsall's starved Syrian face
Has the religious pallor, the blue-socketed eyes
Of a mediaeval portrait.
Betty's bicycle departure
Is in line with the perfunctory lips
Dried and leathered
By long night wakefulness, by blank morning hopelessness.
Mrs Walsall is in love
And has lost interest in everything else.
She wants to dedicate herself, like a sacrifice, to her great
                                                    love.

She does not know how.
She knows she is unacceptably ugly.

54

The child inside her is a growing
Fungus of jealousy
Displacing her from her body. A great hurt,
Like a coulter sewn into her stomach
That she cannot void or vomit.
As Betty rides into the silk-fringed hazel leaves, on the
         chirping saddle,
Mrs Walsall lets the cold tapwater
Numb her hands, and escapes thinking.
She tries to let the water
Numb her body. She fixes her mind
Under the numbing water.
She stands at the sink, numbed.

Doctor Westlake

Has informed Commander Estridge that his elder daughter is indeed dead. Estridge is sitting near the window, small and still, stunned by the event, and by the incomprehensible blunt fact that his daughter was pregnant.

Westlake's delight in such facts, his opportunistic sense of theatre, his lust to uncover the worst and reveal it, could not let the chance pass.

Now Westlake
Has settled his professionally baleful stare,
His congenitally baleful stare,
On Jennifer, who is curled on the couch.
Her words flood and strew
In tangled sweetness and sharp fragments
Like a flower-vase just broken.

Old Estridge is trying vainly to reckon her words up,
As if they were some gibberish formula of huge numerals
Into which his whole family fortune is vanishing.
Explosions from different directions have left him little
                                        more than mere outline.
He props his brow between finger and thumb
And rests his incomprehension on the sunlit pattern of the
                                        carpet.

Westlake, deeply stirred, listens.
The perfumed upheaval of all this ringing emotion and
                                        physical beauty
Is exciting him.
He follows what he can of her cascading explanations.
Her creamy satin blouse, stretching and flexing like a
                                        skin,
Her dark-haired ankles,
Her sandals askew, her helpless uncontrol,
Her giddy mathematics
Which are constructing an abyss –

56

The corpse is absent.
It lies on Janet's stripped bed upstairs, a shape under a
                                                    sheet
Like an article of furniture no longer required, stored
And waiting for removal.

Jennifer is telling
That her sister was in love with the minister Mr Lumb
Just as he had been in love with her
And they were going to disappear together to Australia
Because his religious work had become impossible for him
But then quite suddenly he no longer loved Janet.
Instead he loved herself, Jennifer, much, much more deeply
As he still does love her
And she loves him the same, there is nothing they can do
                                                    about it.
And so she undeceived her sister for her own good and
                                        told her of this alteration
And so Janet has killed herself and that is the extent of it.

Westlake
Keeps losing Jennifer's words
As he gazes fascinated
Into the turbulence of her body and features.
He jerks back into detachment
Noting again, between the inflamed eyelids,
Her irises clear and nimble-delicate as a baboon's,
And the insanity there, the steel-cutting acetylene
Of religious mania.
And immersing himself in her voice, which flows so full of
                                                    thrilling touches
And which sobs so nakedly in its narration,
He is scorched by the hard fieriness,
A jagged, opposite lightning
Running along the edge of it
Like an insane laughter –

Something in his marrow shrivels with fear.

Mrs Holroyd
Is sunbathing in the orchard, between cloudshadows.
Snow-topped blue raininess masses low to the West,
                           bulging slant and forward.
She squints up, calculating whether the bursting bleached
    edges of that mattress are going to wipe out the sun.
The apple trees dazzle. The air shifts and stirs the black
    undershadows, caressing the fur of glow on her throat
    and forearm.
Inside, in the wide white kitchen,
Her husband chews cheese and bread dryly. Makes
                                himself tea.

She watches the honey bees, bumping at apple blossoms,
    groping and clambering into the hot interiors of the
    blood and milk clots.

   In what continues of the sun
she knows she is happy. She is suspended, as in a warm
solution, in the confidence of it. She lies back in her deck-
chair, helpless in the languor of it, just as the chill-edged
sun holds her, for these moments, unable to move.

Her transistor
Bedded in the tussocky moist grass, among milky maids
                              and new nettles,
Squirts out a sizzle of music
And transatlantic happy chat.
She even hums a little, as a melody draws clear,
Letting her round-fleshed, long arm
Dangle behind her head
Over the back of the chair.
She squirms her toes, feeling inside her shoes the faint
    clammy cold of the dew, which will hide all day in the
    dense grass.
She turns her freckled face shallowly
In the doubtful sun

And watches through her eyelashes a dewball jangling its
colours, like an enormous ear-jewel, among the blades.
Closing her eyes
Concentrating on the sun's weight against her cheek,
She lets herself sink.
Her own rosy private darkness embraces her.
A softness, like a warm sea, undulating, lifts her,
Like a slower, stronger heart, lifting her,
A luxury
Signalling to the looseness of her hips and vertebrae,
Washing its heavy eerie pleasure
Through her and through her.

She wants it to go on. She lies there, with a slightly
foolish smile on her face. She wants nothing to change. She
does not want to think about anything, or to open her eyes.

The slow plan of the young corn, advancing
Its glistening pennons,
The satisfaction of the calf's masseter
Moving in the sun, beneath half-closed eyes,
The grass feathering,
The muscled Atlas of the land
Resting in the noon, always strengthening, supporting,
                                                    assuring –

And she is like a plant.
The sun settles the quilt of comfort
Over her sleepy contentment with herself –
Which is like the darkness, secret and happy
Inside the down soft skull
Of a new suckling baby.

Through half-opened eyes, she watches a dark, giant bulk
rocking behind nettles and cow-parsley. Her bull heaves to
his feet. He leans forward, neck buffaloed, tightening his
spine and stretching his thighs, belly deep in the flowering
grass, black under leaf shadow. He sets his neck to a tree-

bole, then jerks up his head, driving it down and jerking it up again, with alarming ease and lightness, scratching his neck and shoulder, while the whole tree shudders. The blossoms snow down, settling along his shoulders and loins and buttocks, like a confetti.

Garten
Is cycling home.
The tatty newsboy's bag over his shoulder
Is swagged with three warm rabbits
And his ferret in its purse.
As he rides he reads the river beside the road.
He hears a cock pheasant and pin-points it on his mental
map
Which is a topographical replica of the region, with each
bramble-stem in place.
A tree-creeper mousing the crannies in the bark of an elm
flags his glance.
Passing the old quarry, he does not fail to see the wet
car-tyre tracks turning inward
From a drying puddle.
Pausing, he queries the concealment of thorns.
He recognises the bicycle. And the van. Hidden. And
hidden.
Now his bicycle is also hidden.
He climbs, behind the quarry rim, through new bracken.
He peers from the crest, between stalks of bracken.
Below him, on a bed of squashed green bracken
The minister sprawls face downward, as if murdered,
Between slender white legs, which are spread like a dead
frog's.
Beside his bald head, Betty's face
Seems asleep under the high clouds.
Her clutching hands have pulled his cassock
Above his buttocks,
And still grip the folds, vigilant in their stillness.
The stillness is dreadful
In the bottom of the quarry.
Till her eyes open
And stare at Garten, who simultaneously
Becomes invisible
To a startlement
That dare not admit him.

Maud
Lumb's housekeeper
Has brought into Lumb's bedroom an armful of
blossoms –
Wet lilac and apple.

Her dumbness
Is a mystery.
Her self-effacement
Is the domestic nervous system
Of this almost empty house.
Her gaze, fixed and withdrawn,
Glaucous, hyperthyroid,
Glisteningly circumscribes
The vicar's needs.

And the full pale mouth
Pursed in a compact nun stillness
Is a sufficiency of speech
Among the ivy shadows.

Her pale hair, glossed back like metal
From the bulge of brow
Concentrates in a tight knob, at her nape.
Her thin throat, her bony Adam's apple
Projects above grandmotherly blacks.

With long, knobbly, bloodless, workaday fingers
She sets the blooms
Either side of the bed's head, in jars.
Smooths from the coverlet petals.
Adjusts the prepared fire of twigs and logs.
Dusts over the long table which already shines.
Pausingly opens
The drawer in the table. She is fitting the key
To the carved bible-box on the table top.
She sits. She is reading a diary.

62

She lifts the lid of a smaller box, disclosing
A glass ball in a black velvet chamber.
This is the hidden treasure.
Her gaze deepens
To the bottom of the dark well in the ball,
Wary, as if the glass might explode.
It is filling with smoke.

And with trampling feet of cattle. It becomes
The swivelling eye of a bull.
Which is broken up by a stag's legs scattering river
shallows.
A stag has backed under a rooty bank,
Chest-deep in the piling robe of river.
Hounds are clinging to it and clambering over it.
A sky-silhouette of grouped down-looking horsemen.
A huntsman wading deep. A swimming hound
Gripping the stag's nose.
The stag's swivelling eyeball.
And now the hunter's knife
Diving into the stag's nape, and a whelm of spray and
limbs

Becomes the billowing foam of a bride,
A girl's face in a veil of ectoplasm
Floating down the church's central aisle, on Lumb's arm.
Their smiles are balanced carefully as they step
Into glare sunlight, as for the camera.
A lumpish form is dodging behind the bride
Who suddenly falls, face downwards, across the steps,
And lies frozen, in the hard sunlight.
A knife hilt is sticking from the nape of her neck.
Lumb's face
Contorts, transforming
To a grotesque of swollen flesh
A glistening friar-fat
Gargoyle of screaming or laughter –

Rending itself slowly, smokily to shreds
Which dissolve in the watery ball's
Simple shining darkness.

Maud puts everything back into the chest
Where Lumb's magical implements lie folded in pelts of
                                                    ermine.
There lies the ebony hilted dagger,
Blade sleeved in the whole pelt of an ermine.

A knock on the door downstairs.
The chest is locked and the drawer closed.
Holding the dagger, Maud comes downstairs.

The breadman wants to know what she wants.
Nothing.
He has to take his slight surprise away with him.
He whistles
Covering his retreat
Into his van and through a swirling turn
Round the dovecot, that hubs the wheel of gravel,
And away.

The doves descend again, dazzling.

Behind the bar

Mrs Walsall draws a half pint, watchfully, for Garten.
His chirpy rat-nervy manner makes her feel deep. He is
being vivaciously familiar with the pensioner under the
window. Old Smayle, who is the vicar's nearest neighbour
at the top of the village, lives with his granddaughter,
Felicity. Garten courts Felicity. Nightly, stormily, un-
happily.

Garten is fishing for the vicar. He is venturing jokey,
overbalancing insinuations, as he sips. Felicity mentions
the Reverend Lumb too often.

Old Smayle defends the vicar.
He admires him. The vicar, he declares,
Has realised that his religious career
Depends on women.
Because Christianity depends on women.
For all he knows, all those other religions, too, depend on
                                                                        women.
What would he do for congregation these days
Without women.
Old Smayle has read it. The church began with women.
Through all those Roman persecutions it was kept going
                                                                        by women.
The Roman Empire was converted by a woman.
And now the whole thing's worn back down to its women.
It's like a herd of deer, he says, why is it always led by a
                                                                        hind?
Christianity's something about women.
His narrowed eye-puffs pierce right to the crux of it.
Christianity is Christ in his mammy's arms –
Either a babe at the tit
With all the terrible things that are going to happen to
                                    him hovering round his head like a halo,
Or else a young fellow collapsed across her knees
With all the terrible things having happened.
Old Smayle's eloquence pours from his travelling library.
His eyebrows arch, hoisting his whole baggy face.

His eyes are seriously amazed
At what such things evidently boil down to.
Something about mothers – maternal instincts.
Something about the womb – foredoomed, protective
                                                    instinct.
Instinct for loss and woe and lamentation.

So men have lost interest. Smayle knows.

Garten has forgotten his own stare.
He is fascinated and out of his depth and wondering
What Lumb is on to.

Evans, the blacksmith, has paid for a half.
He lifts the glass
In fingers that are the masters
Of all the heavy agricultural steel
In the district.
He can be quiet, with a nod.
Betty has come back, looking just as usual.
Garten is disturbed and confused.
He wants to include Evans somehow on his side, in this
                                                    groping.
He watches Betty's high-tension boredom.
He keeps an eye on Mrs Walsall's solemn listening.
He glances from one to the other.
He fancies something is darting between the two,
Escaping him among the crannies of these women.

Evans' wife is vivid and tiny,
Startling, like a viper.
A magnet for local scandal fantasies, spoken and
                                                    unspoken.
Her incongruous Sunday-School cosy chatty manner
Does nothing to tame her deadly glance.
It has the effect of an outrageously lewd cosmetic.
She is Secretary of the local W. I.

What goes on at those W. I. meetings?
The words suddenly blurt out of Garten and he stares
                              after them wildly.
He plunges deeper.
He asks Evans if he's ever read the book of minutes.
He is afraid of Evans. He brazens himself, feeling the
                              eyes of the two women.
He bets that's a book of revelations
Real religious stuff.

Evans weighs Garten with a little easy smile,
A little glance, from little slow wolf eyes.

It would be more interesting, Evans dare say,
To know what's going on, this minute,
Over in Garten's bungalow.
The Reverend Lumb's little van
Seems to have broken down at the gate.

Old Smayle's merriment
Garten's instantaneous exit
And the sun crossing one more degree
Bring the reaching of the landscape roots
A fraction closer
To the vicar's body.

Mrs Garten
Ten years a widow
Is made up at noon.
In the garden hut
She sits back on top of orange-crate rabbit cages
While the Reverend Lumb lifts her into bliss.
The cages creak, the inquisitive rabbits
Try to get a view.
She reaches out to fasten the door's yale
Without losing her advantage.
The flimsy cages start to collapse.
The widow and Lumb sag, clutching at other cages
Which come toppling,
Bursting open, spilling two ferrets,
Creamy serpents.
The widow clings in position, contorted.
Lumb cannot be distracted.
He pushes aside cages, and rabbits struggle out.
Her consternation gazes sidelong at them
From eyes that seem only lightly fixed to her body
Which cares nothing about rabbits
And which Lumb now overwhelms.
He is rapt. His communion
With Mrs Garten is especially deep and good.
She starts to cry out. He urges her cries.

Garten, finding the housedoor open and the house empty,
Hears the sounds.
He runs to the hut door, he kicks at it.
He forces in among the tumble of cages
Which the vicar is attempting to stack.
Mrs Garten is pulling a ferret from under cages.
It is attached to a crying baby rabbit.
She screams at Garten for help.

Estridge's younger daughter Jennifer
Lies on her bed, on her side, gazing into the crook of her
                                                          elbow.

She has sobbed herself stale.
But still hard sighs keep trying to bring relief.
She lies back and watches the clouds.
They are toppling across a snow wilderness.
Stunted fir-trees stoop under drifts.

A girl is struggling across a snow lake
Into the wind.
Closer, closer, the eye runs.
The girl turns, looking back.
The girl is Janet, her dead sister.
And she herself is a wolf, circling her dead sister
And wanting not to be recognised.
She does not want to frighten her poor sister
Who sees only the wolf
Which has followed her a long way
Waiting for her to weaken.
Her dead sister is crying and forcing herself on.
And now turns again, pleading something
But the wind blows the words away.
She watches, with a wolf's interested eyes
Till her dead sister falls.
Now a wolf is killing her where she lies.
Her dead sister lies in the snow.
Her eyes and mouth, already freezing,
Are once again dead.
She starts to howl out over her dead sister who lies in the
                                                          snow.
A wolf crying and snarling jumps up on to her bed
                                                  suddenly
And she screams and jumps upright
In her empty room.

The clouds
Tumble their clumsy bursting baggage

Beyond the window frame
Over the glare, the gloom-dark tree-glitter
Of the day
Where the moments march unalterably.

Dr Westlake

Emerges from his updated, bleak, deserted roadhouse at quarter to one. A brief shower has gone over, loading the greenery. The bluebell-blue cloudmass now huddles to the horizon woods. But the sun soars freely, somewhere behind high parapets, and the black road steams like a vat. He is numb-edged with too much noon alcohol. Dark-edged. He aims himself at his car, parked solitary out on the desert of blue asphalt.

This bulging green landscape oppresses him.
The thick weight behind his eyes oppresses him.

He cannot stop thinking of that dead girl's grey-pink parched-looking lips. The alcohol has dissolved his self-protection, a little. He pauses. His whole body craves pause, and time, like an exhaustion, while he thinks. He feels a great need to think. What was it he wanted to think about?

The air is warm. A nauseous sweet aniseed scent, an over-richness. Like an over-sweet melting sickness in the pit of his stomach. It is reeking from the creamy masses of the hawthorn blossom.

Jennifer's insinuatingly amorous lamenting tones seem to have entered his blood, like a virus, with flushes of fever and shivers, and light, snatching terrors.

He stares at the piled hairy flowers, hedgerow beyond draped hedgerow. Hushed and claustrophobic. He imagines the still Sargasso of it, rising and falling, right across England. Funereal. Unearthly. Some bulky hard-cornered unpleasantness leans on him. He ignores it steadily. He searches for his car-keys, preoccupied, watching the mobs of young starlings struggling and squealing filthily in the clotted may-blossom, like giant blow-flies.

He drops his car-keys in a puddle.
Bending to pick them up
He bumps his bald brow on the car-door handle,

glancingly

But enough to jar off his spectacles
Which drop to the asphalt, where they lie, half-
                                                    submerged,
One lens webbed with cracks.
This awakening into his own world is nevertheless
                                                    satisfactory.
His body is still moving beyond him, its limits blurred.
Getting into the car energetically, with a new grasp of the
                                                    day's course,
He clips the side of his skull, just above the ear,
On the brutal edge of the car-roof.
He sits dazzled with pain
And with rage at the petty error of it, as his eyes water.
He deliberates control –
Carefully cleaning the spectacles, and the cracked lens
                                    especially with meticulous caution –
It flakes out under his thumb, the rim blinks up at him
                                                    empty.
He aligns the spectacles on his nose.
He must insist now, on control
Of every second as it chooses to come.
With firmly applied care, he steers out on to the road.

But he has drunk too much.
And the finality of that dead girl lies at the centre of the
                                                    day
Like an incomprehensible, frightful dream.
And her live sister is worse – all that loose, hot, tumbled
                                                    softness,
Like freshly-killed game, with the dew still on it,
Its eyes still seeming alive, still strange with wild dawn,
Helpless underbody still hot.
For minutes, driving in third gear, Westlake forgets
                                                    where he is.

While what she said about Lumb goes on and on in his
                                                    head
Like a taunt.

72

Because he has known it all the time,
And now he only has to look at it, and there it is.
His wife
And the Reverend Nicholas Lumb
Fit together, like a tongue in its mouth.

His numbness has freed his concentration.
Under this new, naked lamp-bulb
He probes for the deepest nerve of his damage.

He jerks into top gear –
Ending thinking.
His alcohol dullness has settled
To a hurtling lump, a projectile –

He turns in at the gate of his home
With the sensation of finding his trap at last tenanted.

   And the lilac secretness of the drive's curve brings him
suddenly to the vicar's van, tucked up against the back-
porch, almost in under the wisteria drapery.

Westlake's foot presses the lawn verge.
His fingers leave his car door
Just touching its frame but not closed.
He contemplates sabotage to the detestable blue van.
He sidles burglarishly down the side of his own house.

His heart is pounding turgidly, yet he feels light and
                                             separate.
Like a man falling, feeling nothing of the glancing
                                             impacts.
He rouses himself, a deliberate attempt
To realise afresh what he is about.
With his hand on precisely that brick of the corner of his
                                             own house.
He looks at his watch
Where the second hand jogs busily in its ignorant circle.

He watches it, rejoicing absently at the comparative
                                   slowness of time,
And his own freedom in it.
He observes, with a self-mesmerising stillness,
The peeled-back gorges of his rose-blooms, leaning poised
                                      in space.
He marvels again that they are precisely where they are,
Neither an inch this way nor an inch that way,
But exactly there, with their strict, fierce edges.
He moves his head.
Through his unglassed eye, conveniently long-sighted,
He watches the young effortless horses,
Roistering flamily on the slope opposite.
Whole minutes pass.

His feet move. He peers into the grey sterility of his
                                      lounge.
As if he had abandoned it all, years ago, in some
                                    different life.
As if he had just returned, after half a lifetime on the
                                other side of the world.

The front door. The familiar dingy smell of the hall.
He stands at the bottom of the stair.
Weightless, in the balance of decision.

He feels light-headed and inadequate for this preposterous
                                    business
Which nevertheless he proceeds to tackle.
Climbing the stair nimbly
Loading his double-barrelled twelve-bore as he goes
And pocketing other cartridges.

    He pauses just short of the door. He remembers, ab-
surdly, that fully-clothed men jump into the sea for much
less. He explains to himself yet again, more distinctly, and
with a pedantic solemnity of subordinate clauses, that what

he hears is indeed the crying of his wife at some bodily extreme, which can have only the one explanation. But as his brain mounts its annihilating court-case, which will need only the precise, annihilating words, his body has already moved convulsively, and the door bursts open.

At once he sees
That his expectations have been cheated.
His wife is lying fully clothed on the bed.
She is being hysterical in her familiar style,
Rolling from side to side
As if to escape some truth which threatens to scorch her
face.
And the Reverend Lumb
Is sitting at the foot of the bed, considerate as a baffled
doctor.
His calming hand detains her slim ankle.

In one flash Westlake understands
That his accurate intuition
Has been forestalled and befooled
By this goat-eyed vicar.
In spite of what it looks like
Something quite different is going on here,
Even under his very eyes,
And if he could only see clear
Through the vicar's humbug solemn visage
And his wife's actress tragedy mask
It would be plain
That her writhing and cries are actually sexual spasm,
And that the Reverend Lumb, who seems to be gazing at
him
In such cool spiritual composure
And mild secular surprise
Is actually copulating with her
Probably through that hand on her ankle
In some devilish spiritual way.

This crazy idea strikes Westlake like a thunderbolt. And
even if it is not so, even if he cannot actually detect them
performing neck and neck there together in front of him,
that is purely accidental, and as remote as any other co-
incidence, a coincidence inside-out. Anyway, he needs no
proof.

Doctor Westlake levels his gun.
The vicar stands and knocks the muzzle aside.
Dr Westlake swings the gun and knocks the vicar's
                                            cheekbone
With the barrels. The cartridges explode
Tearing the side of the vicar's head, a skin wound.
The two grapple and separate.
The doctor's wife watches, silenced.
The vicar expostulates reasonably and the doctor knocks
                                    him down with the gun.
He fumbles to reload the gun.
The vicar twists it from him and spears it through the
                                                    window.
The doctor runs from the room, down the stairs and out
                                            into the garden,
Retrieves the gun, reloading it as he re-enters the house,
And listens.

The Reverend Lumb's van is turning out at the front.
Westlake runs and from his doorstep fires twice.
One of the van's rear windows goes black
As the van escapes along black rips of gravel.

The doctor spins his gun into the roses.
He pants seriously, feeling for his heart's place and
    staring after the van, squinting as if into the sun's glare.
Huge hammers of blackness reshape him,
Huge hammers of alcohol,
Huge hammers of hellishness and incomprehension.

With a renewed effort of doggedness
He collects the gun, gets into his car, drives away out.
76

Lumb
Bowed at the river's edge, knee in wet gravel,
Washes blood from his face and head, and dabs at the
                                                        wound
With his already bloodied handkerchief.

The wobbling blaze, the sun's reflection,
Brands his retina.
The trees opposite, gargling black water in their drinking
                                                        roots,
Arch over blackly, shifting leaf-hands against the dazzle.
A whirl of radiant midges smokes upstream
Simultaneously smokes downstream
Unendingly.

The throat of strong water in the neck of the pool
Is jabbering a babel, to which he listens.
Voices shut him in.
He sees up through a spiralling stair of voices
Into the sun's blaze cupola.
He recognises voices out of his past.
Peremptory trivial phrases,
Distinct and sudden, behind him and beside him.
One voice is coming clearer, insistent.
It calls his name repeatedly, searchingly.
It is his own voice.
As the other voices thicken over him
He manages, as from his deep listening, to answer: 'I'm
                                                        here.'

The oily backwater, with the sparkle of floatage,
Turns, closely focussed.

He sees a fish rise
Off the point of the long broken finger of boulders
Which pokes out into the lake, from the island.
The lake is oil-still
As if it were pressed flat,

Ponderous-still, like mercury.
The warm weight of thundery air,
Immobile, and swollen with its load,
Hangs ready to split softly.
The tops of the blue pyramid mountains, in the afterlight
Tangle with ragged, stilled, pink-lit clouds
That hang above themselves in the lake's stillness.

Felicity huddles in the boat,
Which rests in the stony shallows.
She is frightened by this enormous cloud and mountain
                              and water stillness.
And by this tiny scrubby island of heather
With its few staringly white birches.
She suggests they row back. It's going to rain. It's going
                                    to be dark.
And this place is awful.
Her own voice frightens her in the vast listening hush.

The fish rises again, feeding quietly off the point.
Then out on the lake, a slap.
Like a shot.
And again, somewhere far out across the great stillness,
                                    another.

The fish rings gently again, off the near point.

He'll just try that fish.

He works out on to the finger, warily, from boulder to
                                    boulder.
She watches his balancing form,
Black against the steely lake, under the electrical nearness
                                of the mountains.
Lightning flutters, orange and purple, in the high silence
Over the peaks, behind the clouds,
And beneath the floor of the lake.

Now he is getting out line.
She looks down at her book, there is just light to read.

Lumb secures his foothold, and lays out a long line and
                                                    waits.
The fish tilts up again, off to the left.
He waits.
It sips again, closer, patrolling its beat.
He lifts his line and puts his big evening fly down in its path
On the lake's glass
Over the pit of hanging mountains and torn, stilled cloud
And quakings and tremors of violet.

Felicity has stopped reading
Though she continues to look at the page.
A little finger of fear has touched her.
Something nudges the half-grounded boat.
She looks up sharply.
Low ripples are coming ashore.
Twenty yards out in the small island bay, the head and
                                        shoulders of a dark shape
Are watching her.

She smothers her fright, telling herself it is a seal.
But now it is moving.
It is coming towards her, still upright.
She sees it is a man.
His ripples crawl away on all sides.
As he emerges to the waist, she sees it is Lumb.
She sees he is naked.
She is astonished, she asks if he went for a swim.
At the same time
She sees Lumb still poised on the tip of the rock, sixty
                                        yards away, motionless.
Again, at the same time, this obviously is Lumb.
Who grasps the stern
And grinning heaves himself naked and streaming into the
                                                    boat.

Yet it cannot be Lumb.
Suddenly she is terrified.
She screams and jumps anyhow out of the boat and
    screaming towards that figure on the point
    she splashes ashore.

As Lumb hears her first scream
Which jerks at the skin of his skull
A black thumb
Lifts out on the water, and presses the fly under.

He fastens into the fish automatically,
And turns.
He sees Felicity stumbling up on to the island,
And a lean leaping figure, moving like a monkey,
Bounding after her.
But it is a good fish
And it runs deep, and he cannot turn it.
Felicity's screams, one after another, procession out
                            across the lake
And jangle against the mountains
As Lumb tries to wedge his rod-butt somehow in among
                            the rocks at his feet.
Till he abandons it with a curse.

He leaps balancing along the rocky spit
And slips and plunges heavily, in over the waist, gouging
                            his thigh, his hip, his ribs
And flounders back on hands and knees, scoring his hands
                            on the granite,
And gets up wet through and hurt.

Felicity and the other have disappeared among the turfy
    hummocks and hollows of the island, among the birches.

He follows her screams into a boggy gulley.
The naked stranger is already dragging her toward the
                            lake.

Lumb brings him down in the shallows and the two
                        wrestle in knee-deep water.
On the painful irregular rocks.
And now Lumb realises
That his antagonist is his own double
And that he is horribly strong.
As they roll together in the water
Felicity gets to her feet and lifts an oar out of the boat.
The two separate and Lumb scrambles to dry land.
His opponent comes close after him and kicks his feet
                        from under him.
Rolling on to his back and looking up, Lumb sees the
                        other standing over him.
His raised arms are poising aloft a rock the size of a baby.
Felicity swings the heavy oar horizontally across the
                        raised arms.
The rock drops on to the attacker's own head and he too
                        falls.
But levers himself up, and sways again to his feet
Doubled over and holding his head, blood spilling between
                        his fingers.

Lumb pulls Felicity away.
They clamber up on to the turf among the birches.
Their feet and knees skid in wetness, and Lumb sees the
                        lake is boiling.
And realises the rain has come
A pressing warm weight on his head and shoulders.
The mountains have disappeared in a twilight mass of
                        foggy rain.
Their pyramids leap in and out of blue-blackness,
Trembling in violet glare, like shadow puppets, and
                        vanishing again.
And thunder trundles continually around the perimeter of
                        the deeply padded heaven
And through the cellars of the lake
With splittings of giant trees and echoing of bronze flues
                        and mazy corridors,

And repeated, closer bomb-bursts, which seem to shower
                                        hot fragments.

Suddenly under a long electrocuted wriggler of dazzle
That shudders across the whole sky, for smouldering
                                        seconds,
Their attacker glistening and joyous
Bounds over the turf bank and on to them.
Laughing like a maniac, he grabs Felicity's arm.
With clownish yells and contortions, he starts dragging
                                        her again toward the lake.
Again Lumb knocks him down and the two men wallow
                                        pummelling,
Plastered with peat-mud, under the downpour.
Finally, gasping and immobilised, they lie face to face,
                                        gripping each other's hands,
One grinning and the other appalled.
Now with twistings and knee-splayings, they strain to
    their feet, still locked, and stare at each other panting.

With a shout the other jerks Lumb off his feet and starts
                                        hauling him toward the lake, like a sack.
Lumb twists to free his hands, freeing his left hand he
                                        grips his own right wrist.
Felicity too hauls on his arm till he struggles upright.
She embraces his waist, together they pull against the
                                        other.

As they wrestle deadlocked, the other begins to gasp with
                                        pain.
Lumb's hand also is being crushed by the other.
He knows his fingers are helpless in that dreadful gripe
Which is bursting his fingertips.
He wrenches to break free as the other
Trying to break away toward the lake
Starts leaping and whirling with unnatural agility
Like a weasel trapped by a foot.
A cramp has locked their grip, hand in hand.

82

With a sudden screech, the other rips free
Holding aloft his stump from which the hand has
                                        vanished,
And uttering long unearthly wails, one after another,
As he plunges into the water.

Lumb tugs to lever up the demonic fingers
Of the torn-off hand, which still grips his own hand.

The other is wallowing in the lake. He rises and falls
And disappears, and rises again, floundering, going out
                                        deeper
Till he disappears at last under the rain-churned smoking
                                        surface
In the darkening blue.

Lumb flings the freed hand out into the lake after him.

Felicity crouches under the bank of the turf.
She is shivering and sobbing, her face abandoned to her
                                        sobbing
As in a great grief.
Lumb embraces her, squeezing her to his sodden body
Under the hammering of the rain, which is now icy,
In the almost darkness.

Westlake's grey Daimler
Rips the road puddles.
It rends hanging holes of echo in the vapour-hung woods.

It slides through the village, slows at the rectory.
Accelerates down burrow lanes, grass-heads lashing the
side-mirrors, as he searches.
Through fir-tree fringes at last he glimpses the blue van,
parked at the house of Dunworth, a young architect, West-
lake's golfing companion.

Westlake is phoning from a booth.

Dunworth, eight miles away in the city, called back into
his office just as he was leaving for lunch, listens to the
voice of his friend.

Dunworth moves fast, surprising himself.

And now his white Jaguar sports is tilting at corners,
flattening in dips and bobbing on crests, breasting the long
straights on a rising note, over the eight miles, as he gnaws
his lips and fights the road's variety.

Westlake's words have supplied the single answer to many
clues.
The warp and weft of hints and suspicions,
Knotted, painfully, laboriously, over a long time, into a
mesh
Have suddenly dragged taut, with the bulk of a body.
A few sprinkled words
Have transformed a bitter-cored ulcer
Into something delicious.

With one glance at the blue van, he walks into the house,
calling his wife's name.
He climbs the fondly designed cedar staircase to his
studio

Without stealth. He returns casually
As if with some curio to show to a guest
Loading his target pistol, with which he is expert,
And without pausing strides into the lounge.

His red-haired wife
Is lying naked on the couch, almost hidden
By the naked body of Lumb
Who, half-twisting, and supported on one elbow, watches
                                                    Dunworth
As if waiting for him.

Dunworth has paused.
His brisk executive plan evaporates confusedly.
The sight in front of him
Is so extraordinary and shocking
So much more merciless and explicit than even his most
                                                daring fantasy
That for a moment
He forgets himself, and simply stares.
He gropes for his lost initiative,
But what he sees, like a surprising blow in a dark room,
Has scattered him.
He raises his pistol meanwhile.
He is breathing hard, to keep abreast of the situation.
He is trying to feel
Whether he is bluffing or is about to become
The puppet
Of some monstrous, real, irreversible act.

He waits for what he will do,
As a relaxed rider, crossing precipitous gulleys
Lets his horse find its way.
He levels the pistol at his wife's face and holds it there,
                                                    undecided.

Her red hair is strewn bright and waterish

Across the arm of the couch which pillows her head.
Her large eyes, mascara-smudged in her gleaming face,
                                        watch him
Moistly and brilliantly.
Her bold, crudely-cut mouth, relaxed in its strength,
Yields him nothing.
He searches her hot fixed look for some sign of reprieve,
Moving his aim from her brow, to her mouth, to her
                                        throat.
She swallows but resettles her head as if to watch him
                                more comfortably.

Her nakedness has outstripped his reaction, incredible,
Like the sudden appearance of an arrow, sticking deep in
                                        his body,
Seconds before the pain.
It cannot unhappen, and now the pain must come.
The white swell of her stomach, welded so closely
To that other strange body, which at first he hardly
                                        notices
But which prints in his brain as something loathsome and
    deadly, a huge python's coils, of some alien nature
    and substance.
He feels a pressure inside his skull, like a long lever
                                tightening a winch.
He sees the pistol out there in front of him
As if it were a fixture he were hanging on to, outside a
                                        window,
Over a night-drop.

His gold hair seems to sweat.
His sunlamp bronze sweats.
His pale-eyed stare is brittle and impotently severe, like
                                the stare of a lizard.

His pistol sinks its aim
Over Lumb's powerful gymnast's shoulders.
The sweat-figured muscles

86

Of the half-twisted torso, and the long sinewy legs
Are an unexpected development.
Dunworth has difficulty
Adding this body to the familiar long-jowled monkish

                                               visage
That watches him unmoving, as if expecting
To see him do something typically stupid.

Those hooded heavy eyes weaken him
Like a load of ironweight.

Dunworth gazes back at his wife
Almost forgetting where he is or what he is doing.
He is helplessly in love.
He stands there, in his child's helplessness,
As if he had searched everywhere and at last somehow he
                                   had found her.
An irresponsible joy chatters to be heard, somewhere in
                       the back of his head, as he gazes at her,
Feeling all his nerves dazzle, with waftings of vertigo,
As if he were gazing into an open furnace.
At the same time he tightens on the butt and trigger of
                       the pistol, readjusting his grip,
As if the terrible moment were approaching of itself.
In the remaining seconds
He studies her lips and tries to separate out the ugliness
                                       there,
Which he remembers finding regrettable.
He tries to isolate the monkey-crudity of her hairline,
Her spoiled chin, all the ordinariness
That once bored him so much,
But he feels only a glowing mass.
He stands there, paralysed by a bliss
And a most horrible torture –
Endless sweetness and endless anguish.

He turns the pistol towards his own face
And puts the muzzle in his mouth.

Lumb is stepping towards him.
Dunworth closes his eyes and tries to clench his strength
Which slips from him like water.
Lumb takes the pistol out of his hand.

Dunworth
Sits in a huddle on the floor.
His eyes, squeezed close, refuse the features of his trap,
Squeezing the ball of tight dazzling blackness behind his
                                                      eyes.
His face is numb as rubber,
His body sunk in a depth of happening which holds it like
                                                  concrete.

The Reverend Lumb has left.
Opening his eyes, Dunworth sees his wife's stockinged
                                        ankles and shoes
Passing close.
When he looks up she is fully dressed and tugging a comb
                                        through her hair.
She ignores him and goes to her room.
He follows and tries the door but it is already locked.

He leans at the door, emptied, merely his shape,
Like a moth pinned to a board,
While the nectars of the white lilac
And the purple and dark magenta lilac
Press through the rooms.

Betty
Naked at her dresser mirror
Is trying to see herself more slender and to look lighter.
And to make certain once again that her breasts
Are no fuller than they were.
Her cat rubs across her bare spine
As she sits on the bed.
She rolls back, hoisting the cat, loving the cat,
Pulls the sheet over her, snuggles to the cat, she dozes.

A bigger hot body nestles in beside her,
Overpowers her, muscular and hairy as a giant badger.
A goblin bald face laughs into hers,
Lifts her to shriek surprised laughter.
He is twisting and squeezing the laughter out of her,
They wrestle in a ball of limbs.

Her whole body is ticklish inside and out.
He laughs like an over-excited dog.
They scramble all over the room,
They crash the furniture, senseless to their bruises.
They roll like wrestlers from one corner to another.
Her shrieks get out of control and abandon her last efforts
                                          of laughter.
Her laughs try to smother her shrieks.

Banging on the door.
Betty peers over the sheet. The cat, sprawled on the
                                          pillow,
Stretches his claws and looks into her face through sleepy
                                          slits.
Her mother peeps in through the open crack of the door.

Nothing is the matter.
Only one of her dreams again. Betty
Makes her face weary-woeful.

Stop sleeping with that cat.

Garten
From shrubbery to bungalow wall, next the window,
Dares full daylight and the watchfulness of many a village
                                        bedroom view
He edges a creeping glimpse, through the window,
Of stockinged feet on a bed.
Is silent in the kitchen
Where a baby breathes in a carry-cot.
Full-length, at the open door of the bedroom,
A yard from the mingling breaths and the working
                                        mattress,
He spies through the crack of the door.
He positions his camera close to the door's edge.
He eases into the open and flashes
What he sees on the bed.

He is striding across the kitchen.
Here is the garden corner, now the hedge hides him.
He whirls in the road.
He pedals calmly past the front of the blacksmith's
                                        bungalow on his bicycle
Without a look back
At the blue van parked outside it.

Exultant, the fuse spluttering in him
Of what he has in the camera.

Felicity

At eighteen, is in her second spring of full flower. Three years ago, a drab child, mongrel and spindly. Today, coming and going among the soft hot-house scents, she is the most exotic thing in the nursery. She is aware of it. She performs it a little, self-indulgently, with a flourish, as a leopard performs its frightening grace.

Her overlong upsweeping nose, her flat calf's eye, her wide reckless mouth, were her father's real ugliness. For the time being they compound her enigmatic triangular beauty.

Gypsy dark skin, intensifying into fierce wire hair. Lusty little moles on her upper lip, and on her cheek.

Slender
She is sliding boxes of bedding plants into the back of a
                                                    Range Rover.
Her dirty heels lift from her sandals.

A five-cornered cacophony, the sand-haired self-elected young Saxon squire, from the Manor at N., claiming Norman prerogative, directs her.

Flirts a little, to excuse his driving gloves.
He daunts her
With brandishings of a voice of colonial polish and cut,
Of military briskness, with brassy fittings,
Demonstrating to all its quelling echoes among the
                                    grouped sullen conifers.
He watches the winking naked small of Felicity's back
Under the grubby red pullover

As she leans forward, sliding the boxes. He observes the skinned patch along two inches of her spine. His thighs bristle. He ponders complacently just what time might drop into his lap in this neighbourhood, with a little shaking of the bough.

His new wife
Is disclosing her vowels likewise, under a wide pink brim,

To the ear of Mrs Davies
Whom she is meeting for the first time.
Mrs Davies
Humours her loonily.
Mrs Davies is the real thing, it appears.
An old sunburned vixen, with a soft belly,
An over-ripe windfall apple
From some lichenous, crumbling lineage
Growing eccentrically sluttish among her potting sheds,
      her seed-frames, her greenhouses, and her compost.
An aged, tatty, unearthed lily bulb
Which secretes some staggering gilded chalice.
A questionable flowerpot troll-woman, her hands half-
                               earth.

Under her silver curls
Which are washed with a faint hydrangea blue
Her full, brown, moist night-time owl's eyes and her full
                    moist lips intrigue her client
Who feels reproached
And styptic, and garish
To hear this unsettling creature
Promoting the home-grown qualities of her assistant.

Felicity has finished. She can go now.
The squire smartly offers her a lift, which Mrs Davies
                    decisively accepts for her,
Reminding the orchid in the hat
To consider the Women's Institute most seriously,
Most, most seriously,
Now that she's living so very near.

   The Range Rover moves away toward face-lifted estates.
Over the engine-din the hat and the squire debate, reso-
nantly, a crisis of interior decorations.

Felicity, looking back, sees
The blue van turning into the nursery.

The driver and his ornament continue to perform, across the length of a tennis court, against international perspectives.

Felicity is biting her nails.

Already Mrs Davies and the Reverend Lumb
Are a bundle of struggling garments,
On the bags of Irish peat, behind the carnations.

Mrs Davies
Agonised ecstatic
As if he were tickling her unmercifully
And he laughing as if he had finally blindfold got her
After months of anticipation
In a dark-house party game.

And they bound, they are flung
With more life than they can contain
Like young dogs
Unable to squirm free from their torturing infinite
                                        dogginess.

Maud
Walks in the graveyard.
She is carrying twigs of apple blossom.
The graveyard is empty.
The paths are like the plan of a squared city.
She comes into the main path.
A woman is walking ahead of her.
Maud follows the woman.
The woman walks to the far end of the path.
Maud does not see her go but now the woman is no longer
there.
Maud also walks to the far end of the path.

She watches a magpie on top of a sycamore.
An urgency, a sucking chak chak.
The magpie flies up and is blown away backwards
By the wind that jerks the grass and passes like a rumour
from tree to tree up the side of the graveyard.
The graveyard is empty.
Maud stands at the foot of the last grave.
A round shouldered stone.
She sticks the blossoming twigs into the perforations of
the green pot on the grave.
The black stone is bare, except for bird's droppings
And a lonely engraved word:
Gaudete.

Maud kneels.
She rearranges some small sea-shells on the grave, which
grub-hunting birds have scattered.
She seems to be praying, She is weeping.

Mrs Davies

Sitting in her potting shed
Is sorting weeds, the fresh, the dried.
Skeletons of many plants dangle in the spider light.
Out of a dusty jar she bounces
A withered goblin midget face
Of fly agaric.
She sets it with other corpses, on newspaper.

Pleasure!
A snake is sliding in over the threshold.
An adder. Pretty! Pretty!
She greets it.
She is prepared – she settles its saucer of milk.
It lifts its head.
It seems to appreciate the caress of her endearments.
Now it sips.
Her singing is comprehensible
Only to the adder, which ignores everything now but the
                                     milk
As she goes on sorting her shrivelled bodies.

The Alsatian

At the Bridge Inn jerks from its drowse, starts barking.
Listens, searches the air, whines, barks.
Goes through from the bar into the house
Where Mr Walsall startles awake in his chair.
The dog is barking at him. It barks at the air.
Mr Walsall reassures the dog but it insists.
He watches the dog,
As it watches him, out of the corner of its eye, urging him
      with more, still more urgent barking.
He gets up and calls for his wife.
He listens. He looks into the bar and calls.
He calls and the dog barks. He looks into the backyard.
Where is she? He asks the dog. He too is disturbed now.
He asks the dog what's the matter. The dog goes on
        barking,
Furiously, as if it were telling him plainly.
Its black hackles stand up, its bark opens a dangerous
       deep note.
It alarms Mr Walsall. He calls for his wife.

His wife is biting a stick.
Animal gurgles mangle in her throat
While her eyes, her whole face, toil
In the wake of a suffering
That has carried her beyond them.
Her head thrashes from side to side among small ferns
      and periwinkles.

Lumb labours powerfully at her body.

Felicity

In her lopsided bedroom has finished packing her splitting
suitcase. Her grandfather, old Mr Smayle, sunk in his pull-
over and face-folds, has anchored his wits in the television.
He does not see her slip out, carrying the suitcase.

She goes up the cinder path of the back-garden, past the
rows of greens, the spill of compost. Birds spurt everywhere.
Fledgeling thrushes launch and fall struggling into under-
growth. Two crows circle low scolding the black shapes that
flounder for balance among the lowest branches.

Clouds crumble, bright as broken igloos. Felicity bends
through a worn gap in the thorn and holly hedge.

At a high creeper-fringed window of the rectory
Maud's face
Dimmed, well back in the room's darkness,
Watches, as if waiting for just this.

Felicity opens the boot of the Vicar's old Bentley. She
stows her suitcase. She closes the boot-lid, with deliberate
care. She returns through the shrubbery and the hedge.

Maud is beside the car.
She opens the boot. She opens the suitcase.
She stares into the suitcase
As into the faked workings of a sum
To which she knows the correct answer.
She hurls the unclosed suitcase toward the shrubbery.
It spins, flinging off its clothes
And falls behind rhododendrons.
Maud embraces herself, as if she were freezing. Her eyes
          pierce through her shiver as through a focusing lens.

Lumb
Is driving along.
He feels uneasy. He keeps glancing round.
At a high bend, over the river,
Stub-fingered hairy-backed hands come past his shoulders
And wrench the steering wheel from his grip.
The van vaults the bank.

He sees tree-shapes whirl, hearing underwood crash, then
                                        shuts his eyes.
He clenches himself into a ball of resistance.
A toppling darkness, a somersaulting
Of bumps and jabs, as if he rolled down a long stair
A long unending way, and again further, then again
                                        further.
Separate and still after some seconds
He realises he has come to a stop.
He stays coiled, afraid to test his jarred skeleton.
Probably the worst has already happened painlessly.
He opens his eyes.
Seeing only darkness, he stretches his eyelids wide.
He relaxes into stillness. He explores a freedom all round.
He feels wetness. He scrambles to his hands and knees,
Imagining his van is in the river, and now beginning to fill,
But realises he is free and out of the van.
He supposes he has been hurled clear. He supposes this is
                                        river water.
He stares into the darkness, trying to split a glimpse
                                        through his black blindness.
But what he thought was river is other noises.
As his head clears, harsh noises din at his head,
Like an abrupt waking,
He makes out shapes in the darkness, confusion of
                                        movement.
He sees heavy rain glittering the night, he feels it.
He sees he crawls on his hands and knees
In the slurry of a cattleyard
Where bellowing cattle lurch in all directions,
98

Topheavy bulks blundering unpredictably, like
                              manoeuvring heavy machinery.
He covers himself from blows
Which are not just rain, which are not kicks and
                              tramplings of the hooves,
But deliberate, aimed blows.
Sticks are coming down on to his head, neck, shoulders
                              and arms.
Bewildering fierce human shouts jab him to consciousness.
He stands and tries to run but the thick sludge grips his
                              feet,
And he falls again, gets up again
Staggering slowly, losing both shoes in the quag.
Shapes of men are hunting him across the yard
Among the plunging beasts
With cudgels, with intent to kill him.
The cattle wallow and skid in the dark,
Their frightened bellowing magnifies them. From a raw,
                              high lamp
Broad sweeping strokes of rainy light come and go,
                              wheeling and thrusting.
He shields his head and tries to see his attackers' faces
Among the colliding masses and tossing silhouettes.
Caught in the flashing diagonals
The faces seem to be all wide-stretched mouth, like
                              lampreys.
They roar at him, as at driven cattle in a slaughter-house.
Their bodies are deformed by oilskins
And their sticks come down out of darkness.

But now they draw off.
Lumb feels a reprieve, a lightening
Though the cattle continue to mill round and press closer
As if still multiplying out of the earth itself.
They are stripping their throats with terror-clamour
But they leave him his space.
He kneels up under the rain.
He shouts to the men.

He tells them who he is, he asks who they are
And what is happening.
What has he done and what do they want?
His voice struggles small in the grievous uproar of the
                                                animals
Which now surge towards him as if helplessly tilted, with
                                                sprawling legs,
And now as helplessly away from him
Like cattle on a foundering ship among overhanging and
                                    crumbling cliffs of surge.

One man comes close, his oilskins flash in the downpour.
He hands Lumb a sodden paper, as if it were some
                                                explanation.
Lumb scrutinises it but can make nothing out in the
                                                broken rays,
As it disintegrates in his fingers, weak as a birth
                                                membrane.

Now the murder-shouts are redoubled
And the malice redoubled. The sticks flash their arcs,
The cattle churn a vortex, leaning together
Shouldering, shining masses, bellowing outrage and fear.
It is like a dam bursting, masonry and water-mass
                                                mingled.
Goring at each other, riding each other,
Heads low and heads high, uphooking and shaken horns,
Plungings as over fences, flinging up tails
And stretched out tongues.
Lumb is knocked spinning, recovers and is again knocked
                                                spinning.
He runs with them, among them, as they circle.
He tries to find a hold on their wet, strenuous backs,
To lift himself above their colliding sides, and to be
                                                carried.
Sticks lash at him, across the backs.

Suddenly everything runs looser.
100

The stampede is flowing to freedom.
He runs half-carried and squashed, and kicked.
Then legs are all round him.
Then he lies under hooves, only hearing the floundering
thunder,
As if he lay under a steadily collapsing building
No longer feeling anything,
From a far light-house of watchfulness, a far height of
separateness
Observing and timing its second after second
Still going on and still going on
Till it stops.

After some time of silence
He draws his limbs to him.
He lies buried in mud,
His face into mud, his mouth full of mud.
Everything has left him, except the rain, ponderous and
cold.
He tries again to remember, through the confusion of
fright,
But it is like trying to strike a match in such rain, and he
gives up.

It is downpour dawn
On a silvery plain of hoof-ploughed mud.
He stands for a while
Feeling the rain, like a close armour of lead, chilling and
hardening.
Not knowing what to do, or where to go now.
He stands spitting out mud, trying to clean his hands,
Letting the hard rain beat his upturned face, letting it
hurt his eyelids.

Now he walks up a slight incline
And finds Evans's body.
Evans is crushed into the mud, as if a load of steel had
just been lifted off him.

101

Near him, Walsall the publican,
His limbs twisted into mud, like the empty arms and legs
Of a ploughed-in scarecrow.
So, one by one, the men of his parish,
Faces upward or downward, rag bodies.

And now he recalls the cattle stampede, an ugly glare of
                                    shock with shapes in it.
Beyond that, his mind dissolves.
He looks at the bodies. No explanation occurs to him.
They are all there is to it.

But now he hears a sharp crying. He looks for it, as for a
                                                    clue.

Ahead, a hare-like small animal, humped on the mud,
Shivers crying,
With long hare-like screams, under the dawn.
It lets him approach.

It is the head of a woman
Who has been buried alive to the neck.
Lumb bends to the face,
He draws aside the rain-plastered hair.
It is Hagen's wife, Pauline.
Her staring eyes seem not to register his presence.
He calls to her, he speaks to her softly, as to a patient in
                                                    a coma,
But she continues to scream
As if something hidden under the mud
Were biting into her.

Near her, sticking up out of the mud,
The red head of Mrs Dunworth
Moves and cries.
She cries through the draggled tails of her hair.
He wipes mud from her mud-spattered mouth but his
                                fingers are still too muddy.

He pushes aside her hair, letting the rain beat down her face,
He presses her brow back so that her face tilts to take the
                                                            rain

He calls to her sharply. She continues to scream
Ignoring him,
And though his hand presses back her face, her eyes still
                                    watch across the plain of mud
As if the last horror
Were approaching beneath its surface.

Nearby
The small soaked head of Mrs Davies
A cry welling from her lips, hopeless,
As from the lips of a child that cries itself to sleep,
While her wide eyes, like pebbles, stare through her thin
                                                          fringe
As if her only life
Were disappearing slowly in the rain-fogged distance.

One by one he finds them.
The women of his parish are congregated here,
Buried alive
Around the rim of a crater
Under the drumming downpour.

And now he sees
In the bottom of the crater
Something moving.
Something squirming in a well of liquid mud,
Almost getting out
Then sliding back in, with horrible reptile slowness.

And now it lifts a head of mud, a face of mud is watching
                                                          him.
It is calling to him
Through a moving uncertain hole in the mud face.
It reaches towards him with mud hands
Seeming almost human.

                                                          103

He slides down into the crater,
Thinking this one creature that he can free.
He stretches his foot towards the drowning creature of
                                            mud
In the sink at the centre.
Hands grip his ankle, he feels the weight.
The hands climb his leg.
He draws the mud being up, a human shape
That embraces him as he embraces it.
And now he looks up for some way out
Under the torn falling sky.

The rain striking across the mud face washes it.
It is a woman's face,
A face as if sewn together from several faces.
A baboon beauty face,
A crudely stitched patchwork of faces,
But the eyes slide,
Alive and electrical, like liquid liquorice behind the
                                    stitched lids,

Lumb moves to climb, to half-crawl
And feels her embrace tighten.
He holds her more securely
And with his free hand tries to dig a hook-hold in the clay
                                    wall.
Her embrace tightens stronger
As if a powerful spring trap bit into his resistance.
He braces to free himself.
Her stitch-face grins into his face and his spine cracks.
Suddenly he is afraid.
He turns all his strength on to her, straining to burst her
                                    grip.
With the heels of his hands he pushes at her face.
She only clamps tighter, as if she were drowning,
As if she were already unconscious, as if now her body
                          alone were fighting to save itself.
And his shouts of rage

Bring to the rim of the crater
Silhouetted against the dawn raincloud
Men in oilskins.

Lumb and the clinging woman are hauled out.
They are carried, still knotted together.
As they go, Lumb fights to keep his lung-space.
Her grip is cutting into his body like wires.

In a flurry of oilskins
He is held down on straw.
Already paralysed, he can no longer move even his face,
As if under stony anaesthetic.
He swoons into and out of unconsciousness,
Vaguely renewing his effort to see what is being done to
                                      him.
Dancing lights and shapes interfere with his sight.
Men are kneeling over him.
A swell of pain, building from his throat and piling
                                  downwards
Lifts him suddenly out of himself.
Somehow he has emerged and is standing over himself.
He sees himself being delivered of the woman from the
                                      pit,
The baboon woman,
Flood-sudden, like the disembowelling of a cow
She gushes from between his legs, a hot splendour
In a glistening of oils,
In a radiance like phosphorous he sees her crawl and
                                    tremble.

But already hands grip his head,
And the clamp of tightness, which has not shifted,
Is a calf-clamp on his body.
He can hear her whole body bellowing.
His own body is being twisted and he hears her scream
                                    out.
He feels bones give. He feels himself slide.

He fights in hot liquid.
He imagines he has been torn in two at the waist and this
                                is his own blood everywhere.
He sees struggle of bodies.
Men are fighting to hold her down, they cannot.

He crawls,
He frees his hands and face of blood-clotted roping tissues.
He sees light.
He sees her face undeformed and perfect.

Blinded again with liquid, but free
He flounders – away, anywhere further away,
On his hands and knees.

And he is crawling out of the river
Glossed as an exhausted otter, and trailing
A mane of water.

He flops among wild garlic, and lies, shivering,
Vomiting water.

At last, pulling himself up by a sapling,
He sees his van, sitting out in a meadow,
Beside the river, under full sunlight.

Figures of men stand waiting round it.
Dazed and dazzled, with trembling legs he walks towards
                                                    them.

But already there is nobody.
Only starlings, seething and glittering among the
                                        buttercups.
With a sudden râle they go up, in a drumming silent
                                            escape.

His van sits empty, the doors wide open, as if parked for
                                            a picnic.

Garten
Has cycled eight miles to the city.
He goes into a chemist's.
Spectacled, heron-crested, Tetley
Splays excitedly
Large glossy prints of badgers in den-mouths
With firefly eyes, among wood-anemones.
Garten is his informer
For the night life and underground activity
Of the woods
And all the secretive operations of birds
Which it is his infatuation
To photograph. Garten is his guide.
The urgency of the return favour
Which Garten now requires
Alarms Tetley, a little.
Can a roll of film be so consequential?

Curiosity blinks through him. His afternoon
Is readjusted.

Lumb
Strips in his room. Resumes
Personal possession of his body
Like a boxer after his fight.

Maud hands him a towel, she pours coffee,
Stokes bigger the log fire, which is already too big.
Positions the high-backed chair, thronelike, in the middle
of the room, fronting the flames.

Lays out fresh clothes on the low bed
Below the window
Which is also a door on to the furnace of the bright world

The chill bustle
Of the blossom-rocking afternoon

The gusty lights of purplish silver, brightenings, sudden
darkenings
Teeming with wings and cries
Under toppling lumps of heaven.

She leaves him.
He half-lies in his chair and lets exhaustion take over.
His only effort now
Is pushing ahead and away the seconds, second after
second,
Now this second, patiently, and now this,
Safe seconds
In which he need do nothing, and decide nothing,
And in which nothing whatsoever can happen.

Garten

Killing time in the city, contemplating the window of a gunshop, sees through the reflection into interior gloom.

Major Hagen is lifting to the light the underbelly detail of one of a pair of collector's pieces. Which he covets. He brandishes the gun, its lightness, with a sudden fury of expertise. Flings it up

To cover a fictive woodcock
Escaping from Garten's hair
Into the free sky above the Cathedral.

Lumb's eyes
Are locked
To an archaic stone carving, propped on his mantel,
                                        above the fire.

The simply hacked-out face of a woman
Gazes back at Lumb
Between her raised, wide-splayed, artless knees
With a stricken expression.
Her square-cut, primitive fingers, beneath her buttocks
Are pulling herself wide open –

An entrance, an exit.
An arched target centre.
A mystery offering
Into which Lumb is lowering his drowse.

Ringdoves are ascending and descending
Between the rectory lawn and the rookery beeches.
And a thrush singing – slicing at everything
With its steely voice
Like a scalpel,
And thrush, lofty, calmer beyond thrush,
And ringdove mulling bluely beyond ringdove
Like treetops, blueing and blurring, stirring beyond
                                        treetops.

Heavens opening higher beyond heavens
As the afternoon widens.

Garten
Strolls in the Cathedral ·
Among rustling tourists and scrambled whispers.
The nervy crowd is blocked.
Some ecclesiastical dignitary,
Mummified senile, bowed nearly double,
Like a Bishop being brought from his tomb
For an important convention,
Supported by two spidery clerics,
Processions shufflingly towards the exit,
Ritualises a whole aisle, his advance
Like an invalid's first inches, his features
A healing, pinkish-purple wound, just
Relieved of its dressings and now airing
In the stained light. Garten stands back. All
Visitors stand back
As from the luckless singled-out casualty
Being nursed towards the ambulance.

Garten sits on a bench, watching the children feed pigeons
and the toddlers chase them.

The uninterrupted sun presses Garten's face. He un-
buttons his shirt, feeling marginally reckless. The winter
tensions ease in his skin. How simple, to vanish. To desert
the whole campaign. The station is two hundred yards.
Emerge in Australia.

A cloud-shadow chills the precincts. He fastens his shirt up.

The prints are ready.

Garten collects them without explanation. Tetley stares
after him as he goes, as alarmed by that caught flash as one
of his own birds.

Evans
Is welding the bar of a harrow.
Sizzling drops of glare fling out
Their wriggling smokes.
The shield-mask lifts away.
The red spot dulls. Evans sees
First Garten
Then the photograph.

He comes erect, waiting for the world to cool
Around the details.
He understands, without too much trouble –
As when he picked up the severed finger end
Under the metal cutter
That what has happened now has happened for good.

But he has escaped it already.
He has stepped that infinitesimal hair-breadth aside
From the point of impact.
He studies the photograph
Like a doubtful bill
Which already he does not intend to pay.

Evans drives. Garten, beside him, explains. Evans drives
calm. Garten cannot believe that Evans is as amused as he
looks. Garten's voice goes on and on, like a bad conscience
protecting itself, against the engine, against the pouring
gardens.

Evans' wife
Is ironing. She sees
Evans' face in the doorway. Her heart
Leaps like a mouse, then hides.
The photograph
Appears, like a burn, on the shirt she is ironing.

Her husband cannot interpret
The foolish abandoned

112

Stupor of her look. She can hear him
Saying something.
Garten is surprised
By a cringe of pity.

Evans' first blow crushes her lip, jolts her hair into a fine
                                                dark veil,
And fixes her in the corner by the fireplace
With angled limbs. She rearranges her slight, small body
Tentatively erect. His questions
Are travelling too fast, and they are not stopping
For her to answer. His second blow
Carries her into the fireplace
From which he snatches her back, as if concerned,
As if to safety.
Now his arm rises and falls, and she bows beneath it.
Garten watches like one whose turn comes next,
Marvelling
At what a body can take.

She is sobbing.
She will tell everything.
Evans stops, without releasing her
From the pressure of his eyes
Smooths down his upcrested hair.
She huddles, small-shouldered, over the bleeding
That drips into her hands.

She starts to tell, coaxed by questions
Which are converted blows.
Her story makes its blurred way, through sobs and
                                                tremblings.
Mr Lumb has a new religion.

He is starting Christianity all over again, right from the
                                                start.
He has persuaded all the women in the parish.

Only women can belong to it.
They are all in it and he makes love to them all, all the
                                                        time.
Because a saviour
Is to be born in this village, and Mr Lumb is to be the
                                                        earthly father.
So all the women in the village
Must give him a child
Because nobody knows which one the saviour will be.

Evans and Garten forget everything, in a ravenous
listening. Even after she has finished Evans continues to
stare and question. It seems he might attack again. She
tells and tells it again. She scrapes out the dregs of telling
it.

It has nothing to do with loving the vicar.
She doesn't love him.

Though poor Janet Estridge was infatuated with him and
so is her sister and so is Pauline Hagen and Hilda Dunworth
and Barbara Walsall and her and her and her and her, it's
true, all those are infatuated with him

But she doesn't love him at all.
She doesn't even like him. He frightens her.
She doesn't know how she got into it, she only wishes she
                                                        was out of it.
He must have hypnotised her, she is sure he did.

Evans turns from the revelation
Radiant with incredulity
Like a bar of furnaced iron. He meets Garten's eyes.
Garten has no chance to move.
His brain moves, but his body is too late to catch up.
Then his long hair lashes upward,
His jawbone jars sideways,
The amazed loose face-flesh jerks at its roots.

114

His limbs scatter, like a bundle of loose rods.
He falls into a pit.

    The pattern of the oilcloth returns slowly, magnified, and close to Garten's eye. He feels its glossy cold on his cheek. He retains the snapshot picture of Evans' fist in the air.

    But Evans has disappeared. Mrs Evans is hurrying out, putting on her coat. She leaves the door wide.

Garten half-lies
Retching. He vomits
On to the oilcloth
Of the blacksmith's kitchen.

Maud
Is doing something with a white pigeon.
It balances on her folded fingers, as she carries it into the
                              bare, bare-boarded room.
Maud's face is closed
Like a new mother's over her baby's first suckling.
She kneels on the bare boards.
The pigeon flaps up, glide-flaps
Sinuously round the room, returns to the floor
Between her hands, wobblingly walks.
Its tilted head studies her, its pink eye. It blinks.

In the room above
Lumb's head has sunk sideways.
He is not sleeping.
His eyes, fixed, seeing nothing, direct their non-gaze
By accident of his neck's angle
Toward the carpet.
His lips loll idiot loose. His mask
Is loosened, as with ultimate exhaustion.
His fingers wince.

Maud, in her bare room below, has wrenched the pigeon's
                              head off.
Her blood-smeared fingers are fluffed with white down.
Now her hooking thumbs break the bird open, like a
                              tightly-taped parcel.
Its wing-panics spin downy feathers over the dusty
                              boards.
She is muttering something.

Lumb's mouth lumps with movement.
Sounds lump in his squeezed throat.
His lungs struggle, as under water.
His leg-muscles, his arms, jerk. His hands jerk.
Unconscious he tries to get up
As if a soul were trying to get out of a drowning body.

116

Garten

Stands at the door of Felicity's cottage. The body and ripening hair of a dense honeysuckle bush the lintel. Over there, the rectory windows, among the virginia creeper and behind high massed hollies, look ordinary.

Felicity's face, in the gap of the door, offers nothing. She lets him come inside. Out of the observation of the village. In the cramped, coat-hung hallway, their whispers conflict.

Her grandfather, keeping his eyes on the television, shouts his enquiry. Garten bends a smile awkwardly on to his greeting, shouted back.

She wants him to go. She doesn't want to talk any more.
It's finished. No, it is not finished.
He is insistent. She is insistent.
The photograph
Is suddenly there. His weapon.

Behind her face, which registers no change,
Everything changes.

And Garten feels the freedom, for a moment, to take his bearings unforgettably on the stuffed fox-head, and the grandfather clock, touching quarter to four.

Then her glance frightens him.

Solemn
As a person
After the doctor's terrible look, she
Puts on her coat.

Maud
Is standing naked.
She is sponging herself with the bunched rag of the
pigeon's body.
She is painting her breasts,
Her throat and face, her thighs and belly,
With its blood.
Swaying her head, she continues to paint herself
Whispering more rapidly and sobbingly, more absorbed,
As if she were crazed,
As if she were doing something crazy
With the body of her own child.

Lumb's head is pulsing pain.
He becomes aware, he tries to raise his hands to it
And to open his eyes,
And to get up.
He manages to glimpse flames.

He sees
A distant volcano.
It is not a volcano, but a hill.
He sees a church-shape, a silhouette Cathedral
On top of the hill.
He sees, with difficulty, a river of people
Flowing up the hill.
It is like a marching of ants.
It is a river of women
Flowing up the hill
To the Cathedral.
They are crushing in through the great West open doors
of the Cathedral.
Bodies cram the doorway, in pain,
In struggle,
Stricken and driven faces and reaching hands, seen with
difficulty.

In the fog of his vision
Which clears

118

To the dull tolling of a drum, a slow, convulsive pulsing
As if the whole stretch of sky were the drumskin.
Women black as flies
Like women mobbing for names
At some pithead disaster, mobbing to see bodies and
                survivors, to hear the good news, the terrible.
They pile into the Cathedral, which is already packed,
Almost climbing over each other,
Pressing towards the high altar,
Raised faces, crying towards the altar, and arms lifted
                          towards it
Like swimmers from a wreck,
As if the Cathedral were sinking, with its encumbering
                mass of despairing women,
As if that altar were the only safety,
As if the only miracle for them all were there.

Their noise is a shrill million sea-bird thunder.

Felicity
Walks in the graveyard with Garten.
Among decayed bouquets, unsheltered stones, neglected
                                                    grass.
No, she does not want to examine the photograph more
                                                    closely.
Near a comfortless sycamore
Garten studies it.
He is a little tipsy with the power of his new role.
A cuckoo, too near, moves its doleful cry from tree to
                                                    tree,
On and on and on.

He tells her, as if he were splitting logs cleanly,
What he has seen today.
And what he is going to do with this evidence.
She snatches at it, to tear it.
He protects it. He mocks,
He lets her taste his exhilarated bitterness.
He shows her the picture, guardedly,
As if spotlighting her eyes with a mirror,
As if searching there
For some mark of mortification.

Her frustrated hands
Claw repeatedly.
Garten's cheek whitens, roughened, an opened grid,
Then gleams blood.

Felicity is running toward the gate.

The Cathedral
Is rumbling, as if it moved slowly on its foundations.
It is humming the chord
Of all those cries' and the drum-pulse.
It is itself throbbing like an organ.

And the capacious cavern of it
The stalactite forest of walls and roof
Reverberates,
Magnifying their throats.

The tall altar candle-flames tremble
In the pulsing air.
Above them, above the altar,
Swathed in purple and gold,
Lumb
Looks down on to the tossing sea of faces,
The blighted and beseeching expressions,
The strangled eyes and grievous mouths,
Futile-seeming tendrils of fingers
That stretch their pleas towards him
Inaudibly
In the thunder of the one voice
Of all the voices
Beating like massed wings.

Throned beside him
An apparition, a radiance,
A tall blossoming bush of phosphorous
Maud has become beautiful.

He leans among the candle-blades towards her.
She raises her face to his.
The supplications intensify. The hammering voices
Make a walled deafness,
A peace like a cave under a waterfall
In which he kisses her mouth.

The drumming
Sharpens to a banging
And the cries
Harden like lament, like black disgorging smoke
                    reddening from the roots into oil-flame
Breaking in on the kiss,
And the candletongues
Lengthen leaping as if these new cries fed them,
And now thickening their flames with the flaming
Of her whiteness
And with the flames of his purple
As if these two were petroleum.
He embraces her. Their kiss deepens.
In a bush of flames they are burning.

The Cathedral
Oozes smoke from every orifice
Like a smouldering stack of rubbish.
Smoke bulges unrolling
From the shattered-out windows,
From the doorways.
Flames lance out, broaden and fork upwards
In rending sheets and tatters.

But the piling of women
Does not cease to spill into the interior,
Under the out-billowing smoke,
As if women were fuel
Enriching the conflagration, angering the flames
That claw for the sky,
Hooking upwards, clenching about the Cathedral
Like talons
Of a giant dragonish gripe.

As if the Cathedral
Were being crushed in the upreaching foot
Of an immense upside down griffon
Which is falling

Into a crater of black smoke
The griffon being aflame,
Beating deeper and deeper,
A star of struggling rays,
A glowing spot
Muffled away
By the banging –

Till only a hard banging remains.

Lumb
Lies unconscious on the carpet, face crawling with sweat
In front of the burned-out fire.

Maud
Striped with the dove's blood, which has now dried,
Lies face upwards on the bare boards
Of the room beneath, still gripping
The blood-rag of the bird.

Her eyes flicker open.

She listens
To the banging on the door downstairs.

Felicity

For a moment can make nothing of the blood-smeared brow, cheekbones and throat in the crack of the door opened three inches.

Maud studies the weak pretty face, which is trying to interpret her sheet-draped nakedness, as the door widens.

Felicity has to speak to Mr Lumb. Very urgent. Maud's smile seems to understand, as she steps back and lets the tear-flurried face surge past her with its agitation.

So it is that Lumb, opening his eyes, finds Felicity staring down at him.

He springs up. He is cleansed and renewed.
His arms close round her, as if joyfully.
At once she is crying freely.
She feels his embrace is safety and assurance.
She tells him everything
About that picture and about Garten.
Already she can hardly believe any of it.
She prays it was faked.
She begs him to tell her it was faked.
He tells her it was faked.
His laugh frightens her, but she grasps it as more
reassurance.

She tells him she has put her suitcase in the back of his car, just as they said. She wants to leave now, this moment. Why can't he just cancel that meeting tonight.

He kisses her, overpowering her with his kisses and easy
smiles.
He starts to unzip her dress.
She stops him with hard fingers.
She wants him to save it
Till they have escaped right away from all this and from
everybody.
Till they are alone together, absolutely together.
Why can't they go now?

124

When he will not be stopped,
Explaining without explanation that he cannot cancel the
                                                    meeting

Because he simply cannot
She suddenly announces
That she is coming to the meeting, too,
So she can see for herself,
So she can be completely sure
That the rumour about those meetings is a lie.
That will prove everything to her.
And she needs it to be proved.
She is suddenly strong.
She realises she is strong.

She adds something else:
She is never going home again.
Lumb
Gazes blankly toward a reassessment
Impossibly beyond him. Two worlds,
Like two strange dogs circling each other.

   The door opens, and Maud stands there. Lumb asks
Maud to look after Felicity and prepare her for the meeting.
And to instruct her. They will introduce her to the Institute.

Felicity
Looking at Maud, and looking again at Lumb
Reasons herself scramblingly
Out of the sudden terror
The light electrical gust
That grabs at her, to rush her
Away from this house,
Away from these two –

She takes firmer hold of her new initiative.
She goes out with Maud.

Holroyd

Though it is after five, is in his cattle yard with his man and the vet. They are sawing the horns off a young bull. Its hooves slam, its muscular half ton convulses, like a fist, racketing the locked steel bars of the crush, as the three men strain, two of them levering the head far over to one side, and Holroyd, his full weight leaning backward, sawing with a wire.

Seeing his wife climb into her car, and knowing where she is going, Holroyd shuts his mind from her, grimacing like a face in the dentist's chair, as he concentrates on the rip of the wire, the angle of his double punching pull, and the ammonia smoke of the horn burn.

The bull roars long and horribly, like a tiger. The horn pulls loosely over and off, heavy. Nimbly the vet tweezers for the cut end of the vein, that showers him with a rigid thread of blood. He twirls the tissue to a knot. He sprays smoking purple antiseptic into the blood-streaming skull-crater, while Holroyd stands back, crimsoned and panting.

But now as they grip the bull's nose-ring, and lunge into wrestling and levering the surviving horn upwards, Garten appears beside Holroyd.

Garten is an agricultural pest.
But he is coming closer, not answering Holroyd's query.
He is holding out the photograph, like a peace-offering.
Holroyd has taken it, lifts it.
In spite of himself, his eyes are fascinated.
His mystification narrows.
He is wondering why Garten presents him with this
                                    questionable picture.

The horn stands ready for the wire, which dangles in curls from Holroyd's preoccupied hand. The two men, with locked joints, and full strength at full strain, have pinned the dangerous weight. The bull's gruelling roar vibrates the concrete of the yard beneath their boots. Garten is saying something.

126

Holroyd's dignity has stiffened. A big florid man, with handsome brown eyes and silver curls.

He glances at Garten, flushed and stormy and full of hatred. He responds to nothing Garten says, and hands him back the photograph as if it were of no interest.

He returns to his bull. The animal's uplooking eye squirms like a live eye in a pan. It emits a yodelling weird roar, like a steel roof being ripped by a power saw, as the wire bites.

Estridge

Is looking right through the photograph to his unburied daughter and the stump-raw amputation of that morning's event.

He is sharply aware of his age. The recurrent idea to kill Lumb keeps foundering in the proliferating concerns for what ought rightly to be done, in a civic and rational manner. Apart from taking council with Hagen.

And what is this other strange tale, this new religion? Something diabolical, concocted, filthy, very possible. A lecherous priest and a gaggle of spoofed women. Hysterical bored country wives. Credulous unfortunate females.

Evans is giving his simple statement. Evans, it seems, intends to walk into the church basement tonight and see what's going on at the W. I. meeting. Anybody else will be welcome. But nobody must think they're going to restrain him, when he meets Mr Lumb.

Looking at Evans' dangerous, thick-set face, Estridge feels the draughty lack of his uniform. He feels the sheer-fall possibilities of being left out. But mostly he feels age, the wrinkle-crisp caul of the life-husk, an inert scratch-numb detachment. It would be so easy now to do nothing.

But then the sudden raving fantasy comes
Like a lump of insane music
Pulping Lumb's skull with an axe

And Estridge's heart bounds again and flutters.

Estridge and Evans

Drive into the gravelled court behind Hagen's house, circling the old well which is surmounted by a looted Silenus, decorated with fantails. Mrs Hagen, negotiating the grass-verge, drives out past them without a glance.

Hagen's man is holding a tall bay mare by a snaffle. Hagen, leaning his chest against a steel gate, watches the slender sooty stallion descending from its horsebox, on powerful springs, restrained by an insect-thin manager.

The too-heavy clay of Hagen's face is sagging as the day lengthens. His eyes are fixed in a spiritless nicotine-yellow dullness. Estridge, coming beside him, hands him the photograph without a word, casually as a cigarette.

Then stands watching the flashing ballet of the two horses, as they touch noses and flare tails, like great fish, like yachts.

Hagen, absorbing the photograph, massages his brow between thumb and forefinger, as if resting. The stallion whinnies, a squealing barrel-echoing snigger, as he feels his power swell, glitteringly, in the odours of the mare.

Hagen is contemplating the photograph, which seems very satisfactory, as if it were a just-completed jigsaw. He lifts his brow, to raise his head slightly, letting his whale's eye, small and cold, rest on Estridge. He is thinking: so it is proved, and now they want me to do something about it.

Taking his old friend's arm, he leads him toward the house, as if to impart something even worse. Their old wars go with them, cleaned and simplified, under the glare sunlight.

Evans, a grin stuck on his face, watches the stallion sprawling on the high mare, like a drunk on a table.

Estridge's shout interrupts.

Garten

Leans his bicycle on a low wall, between Westlake's car and Dunworth's, and goes straight into the house. He pauses, surrounded, as by sudden guards, by all that polished modernity, the positioned furniture, in ultra colour, designed by Dunworth himself, like the demortalised organs of a body.

Through and beyond, framed against the panoramic feature window, he sees the two men sitting, a whisky bottle between them on a low table, and glasses in their hands.

Dunworth is discussing killing himself, which is what he seems to consider appropriate. Westlake does not say what he thinks. He makes provisional noises.

Their sentences
Falter and evaporate.
Bottomless silence drinks their ideas.
They are trying to imagine logicality.
Neither can quite feel the seriousness of their own words
                                        or of the others.
They stare out, like yarded beasts, across the blue-
                        layered monotony of the distance,
And sip.
They feel gently around in the illusory emptiness of these
                                                minutes,
Which are passing with such crowded rapidity.
They are quietly aghast
At the certainty that sooner or later they will have to move

Westlake is afraid that when he moves he will do
                something barbarous, disproportionate, insane.
Dunworth is afraid that if he is left alone he might well
                kill himself in a light-minded effort to be sincere.
Westlake hunches hooded in tortoised concentration,
                        behind his dark-rimmed spectacles.
Dunworth's face is exposed and woebegone, like a
                        beggarwoman's at a crossroads.

130

Garten introduces the photograph.

With one glance Dunworth has seen too much. Now he only wants to escape right away, fast enough and far enough for all this to disappear in slipstream and exhaust. He wants to lie down and sleep for fifty years in some utterly different landscape, and wake up in another age.

Westlake stares into the photograph as into a culture under a microscope.

Dunworth paces about the room. He can feel the whole day slipping like some horrible landslide, towards a brink. Everything is on the move, everything inside this house is on its way to the brink, the house itself, everything in the garden and those trees, it's all on the slide. Even the clouds. The whole day. And himself in the middle of it, helpless.

His skin panics with hot and cold draughts
As Westlake stands up.

Women
Are assembling in the church basement.

Mrs Davies is in charge of refreshments. Mrs Evans
follows her instructions. Dainty triangular sandwiches,
prettily stacked. Tinned salmon, liver paste, cucumber,
lettuce and tomato.

A hushed animation, sombre and uneasy.
Something is wrong and everybody is aware of it.
It is not only the gossip funeral for Janet Estridge.

Mrs Davies peels a blue razor blade from its wrapper.
The glans of a withered fungus
Receives its edge, and releases slices
Into each of three sandwiches.
Mrs Davies sets these apart.
Mrs Evans is pouring a milky liquid from a medicine
                                bottle into the tea-urn.

The loudspeakers cough and clear their throats at the
                                corners of the ceiling.
Betty has put a tape on the stereo.
Suddenly the women are engulfed
Under archaic music of pipes and drums,
An inane cycle of music, hoarse and metallic.
Mrs Davies is setting out cigarettes of her own blend.
Plates of sandwiches circulate and trays of cups of tea.

The birdlike agitation of women, fussy, tense, watchful,
                                thins
As the music works behind their faces
And a preoccupation deepens.
A snaking coil of smoke materialises.
Already their eyes are glazed like young cattle.
They are waiting for the first shiver of power.

Something is obstructing it.

A difficulty, the power will not flow.
The music is tangling with some obstacle.

Everybody is here, except Maud. And the Master.
Jennifer
Knows more and more clearly that she should not have
                                                    come.
Mrs Evans shuts herself up in busyness.
Women in groups wait nervously for things to warm up.
Mrs Dunworth sits with the doctor's wife and Mrs Hagen
A little apart,
Like three asked to stay behind after the doctor's tests –

All are quiet with something like fear –
Nearly a definite prickle of fear.
Like passengers in an aircraft, just as it lifts off the
                                                    runway,
Hearing a peculiar note in the engine.

Betty turns the music up purposefully.

Maud
Is ready.
Black lace in her hair,
But under her black shawl
A long dress of white satin, a bridal dress, flashes as she
moves.
Felicity is sitting with brilliant eyes, at the kitchen table.
The drink Maud served her
Has made her ears ring. Her lips feel numb.
Her fingertips feel enormous.
She is waiting to be conducted to the meeting
And sits watching Maud fixedly.
It occurs to her
That Maud's regalia is some special craziness
Connected to her dumbness.

Lumb promises to follow within minutes.
Felicity appeals with a last look.
Words seem suddenly too big, they refuse to shape in her
mouth.
She interprets his look as reassurance.
Actually his face is impenetrable.

Now as Felicity follows Maud out
She takes a deep breath, and for a moment has to pause
For the sudden smouldering fire under her midriff.

She sees the church.
It looks like an evil black shape painted on a wall.
Simultaneously she remembers that she left no note for
her grandfather.
She is heavily aware of her lips, lying together as if they
were swollen
And of the inner surface of her thighs brushing together,
as she follows Maud.
She feels Maud's madness in that processional stately
walk, flashing whiteness,
As they go among the graves.

134

Lumb
Is cramming books into a trunk.
He crams in clothing.
Among the clothing
He nests, with hurried care,
His magical apparatus.
He lifts the stone woman from the mantel
And settles her snugly among underclothes.
He searches in the box, in the drawer –

Something is missing. His dagger is missing. His weapon
                                                    of weapons.

He scrabbles, he unearths – vainly. He listens.

He knows
It is not in this room.

Maud
Enters the church basement, pausing impressively
Like a slightly tipsy actress.
Maud is impressive in her get-up – and frightening.
Felicity is frightened
Seeing so many confusedly familiar faces
Looking unfamiliar
As if police held her.

She meets Mrs Davies' mystified savage look
But it is Mrs Davies' welcoming smile,
Her surprise of affection.
It is Mrs Davies' arm round her shoulder
Guiding her among the confusion of women, the harsh
            music, and all the movement of hands and faces
Which numb her every second more deeply.
Vaguely she looks round for Maud.

Maud is already poised motionless at the corner of the
                                        rectory.
She is watching Lumb.
He is lugging his trunk out though the back door.
After backing his car up, he tilts the trunk into the boot,
            closes the boot, and returns into the house.

Maud is crossing the space of gravel.
Passing the open car-window her arm dips inside, and she
                                        goes on
Round the far corner of the house.

Half-way across the graveyard, she hesitates at a freshly-
dug not yet occupied grave, and dropping the ignition keys
between the covering planks, goes on toward the church.
    Lumb is making a last furious search through his room,
ransacking drawers and cupboards.

In the bar at the Bridge Inn

The assembly of husbands and their sympathisers,
          muffled by ceiling and walls and cigarette smoke,
Is a squabble of unlistened-to voices
Trying to become a meeting.
Mr Walsall continues to draw and push forward the
                              required drinks.
The photograph lies on the bar.
Garten sits near it, watching over his property, installed
                    in the focus of excitement.
Evans keeps his print concealed, he has had enough of it.
Behind backs and elbows
Dunworth repeatedly tries to introduce a fuddled
                         reasonable attitude.
His mouth moves soundlessly in the din.
Westlake is saying nothing, he listens to everybody
Keeping his own thoughts untangled.
Holroyd in a big consoling voice wants to see proof
Because a photograph is not really proof.
He for one can't believe it's quite as lurid as everybody
                         wants to think.
And he's not going to commit himself till he gets facts.
As for going up to the church, he can't see what that will
                         prove at all.
A shout of voices swamps him,
Complicating and simplifying the possibilities, faces are
                    jerking and heads.
Full pints stream over boots, glasses tilt empty and
                         waiting,
As Walsall's arms move steadily.

Nobody quite knows what to do.
They continue to drink more forcefully in search of
                    definition and action.
They all know what they want to happen
And they drink to make it more likely
So that the criss-cross push and pull of voices works
                    steadily in one direction.

137

Evans keeps hauling the tangle into a tight hard knot and
                                    humping it further.
When they hear his voice, everybody listens.
As he gets drunker, his memory becomes more naked and
                                    ungoverned.
He feels more and more his strength, feeling more and
                        more the weakness of the others.
His little eyes become deadlier.
He gleams with impatience to do the direct, conclusive,
                                    simple thing.
He has anaesthetised all thought of consequences.

Only old Smayle, behind backs in the corner,
Keeps his humour – as amazed, nevertheless,
As he is amused.

Lumb

Is walking in a circle. The room is a maze of smoke
From smouldering piles of herbs in ashtrays.
He is holding something up, it is a stag's antlered head on
a pole,
Heavy and swaying and shag-maned.
The pipe and drum music is a tight, shuddering,
repetitive machine
Which seems bolted into the ground
And as if they were all its mechanical parts, the women
are fastened into it,
As if the smoke were the noise of it,
The noise of it raucous with the smoke and the smoke
stirred by it.
A hobbling, nodding, four-square music, a goblin
monotony,
The women in a circle clapping to the tread of it.
Their hair dangles loose, their eyes slide oiled, their faces
oiled with sweat
In the trundling treadmill of it.
It is like the music of a slogging, deadening, repetitive
labour.
They have left their faces hanging on the outside of the
music as abandoned masks.
They no longer feel their bodies.
They have been taken deep into the perpetual motion of
the music
And have become the music.

Now Lumb pauses
Confronting one of the women as if at last he had been
directed to her.
She has stopped clapping and she waits, helpless, as the
music intensifies –
But it is not for her, and he leaves her, she is gathered
back into the music.

He weaves among the women and the smoke,

139

Pausing here and there, in front of one woman then
                                             another.
The clapping grows harder, sharper, it is like the
                                   slamming of wood slabs
Of hands that are no longer hands.
The women are stripping off their last clothing as if to
                            cool and liberate their limbs,
To work more freely in the gruelling trial of the music.
Their feet are trying to climb the music but are too
                                          heavily rooted.
The music is like all their heads being shaken together in
                                                  a drum.

Felicity is standing loose, hardly moving,
Her eyes far off.
In the lottery of the mushroom sandwich
Everything was arranged for her.

What she has eaten and drunk
Is flying her through great lights and dropping her from
                                            gulf to gulf.
Wings lift through her and go off.
A tiger
Is trying to adjust its maniac flame-barred strength to her
                                                   body.
And it seems natural
That she should be gazing at the surprisingly handsome
                                                  breasts
The surprisingly young body of Mrs Davies,
And the luminous face which is now revealed to her as an
                                     infinite sexual flower.
She can see Mrs Davies is infinitely beautiful
And Mrs Garten is a serpentine infinite wreath of flowing
                                                    light.

Inside Felicity a solid stone-hard core of honey-burning
                                    sweetness has begun to melt
And she knows this is oozing out all over her body
140

And wetting her cheeks and trickling on her thighs.
The sweetness is like the hot rough fur of the tiger as it
                                    bulges and bristles into presence,
A hot-throated opening flower of tiger, splitting all the
                                    leafy seams of her body,
And Mrs Walsall's bony frame is revealed to her as an
                    Egyptian cat-headed goddess on an endless plain
Swaying in tall flames, with a sparkling city in the
                                    distance beyond her.

Lumb is suddenly standing in front of her looking at her.
He is holding something shaggy and terrible above her.
Felicity understands that she is a small anonymous
                                    creature which is now going to be killed.
She starts to cry, feeling the greatness and nobility of her
                                    role.
She starts to sing, adoring whatever the terrible lifted
                                    thing in front of her is,
Which needs all she can give, she knows it needs her.
She knows it is the love animal.
The clapping hammers her head, her body has given up
                                    trying to move.

Now she becomes aware that Lumb is holding some
                                    slender thing towards her.
He touches her navel with it, it seems to her to be a
                                    foxglove.
Fleetingly she cannot understand how she came to be
                                    naked.
But it is too late to do anything about anything.
She is already drowning in the deep mightiness of what is
                                    about to happen to her.
She knows she herself is to be the sacramental thing.
She herself is already holy
And drifting at a great depth, a great remoteness, like a
                                    spark in space.
She is numbed with the seriousness of it, she feels she is
                                    vast,

Enlarging into space from a withering smoulder of petty
                                                    voices.

She touches the wand, which is actually of twisted
                                leather, and moves as he leads her.
The clapping no longer uses human energy.
It is like the steel oiled parts of the music,
Like a generator
Pulsing radiance into her, solid and dazzling, fringing her
                                whole body with flame.

Somehow she has become a goddess.
She is now the sacred doll of a slow infinite solemnity.
She knows she is a constellation very far off and cold
Moving through this burrow of smoke and faces.
She moves robed invisibly with gorgeous richness.
She knows she is burning plasma and infinitely tiny,
That she and all these women are moving inside the body
                                of an incandescent creature of love,
That they are brightening, and that the crisis is close,
They are the cells in the glands of an inconceivably huge
                                        and urgent love-animal
And some final crisis of earth's life is now to be enacted
Faithfully and selflessly by them all.

In the smoke-filled basement
The faces, the smoke, the clapping, are a tunnel
Down which she steps with Lumb
Her outstretched fingertips touching the wand
Towards the waiting unmoving figure of Maud.

Estridge
Has left Hagen in his study.
Hagen disdains to squander his dignity.
His face-shield, armorially quartered,
The monument of hurt, no longer a nerve,
Leans over trays of butterflies.

To make up for the lost Major, Estridge's purposeful rage
redoubles itself, remembering that Hagen has gone through
little enough yet, while he, Estridge, is an incinerator of loss
and pain. His dead daughter, her living sister, what is left
of his own life, make one flame, overpowering his dust and
sticks and papery tissues, a glowing fullness of energy,
extraordinarily comfortable. He does not know what he will
do now. He knows that anything will have to be forgiven
him.

He enters the Bridge Inn for the first time in his life,
remembering, as he pushes the door, the wren in Macbeth.

His arrival
Is like permission: it flings open all limits.
His ferocity, concentrated in that bulbous hawk's eye,
Delegates, as in a battle,
A legitimate madness to each member.
Glasses drain into flushed radiant faces.
Evans,
Feeling himself the key in the log-jam, moves.

They all march in a tight group up the middle of the
evening street. The dry prattle of their herding feet brings
faces to windows and doors.

They are solemn, possessed by the common recklessness,
not speaking above the odd murmur. Overawed by their
own war-path seriousness. In the armour of alcohol, they
feel safe. And new satisfactions open. The single idea of
revenge shuffles its possible forms. Now Lumb will some-
how pay for everything. Their decision has released them.
It has outlawed him. Sentenced him. All they have to do is
carry out the sentence.

143

A straggle of boys trails along,
Touched by the thunderish atmosphere of evening
                                        catastrophe,
The mood of disaster,
With thrushes washing their voices in the gardens, and
                                        beyond,
And pigeons soothing each other,
And the flame-burdened laburnums shedding their blue
                        shadows on the pavement,

And the dark phalanx of men close together,
Like a mob of prisoners being taken to execution,
Past the garden gates, the open doors,
Led by an Alsatian
That leans all its lunging weight on the air,
Scrabbling to bound forward, and coughing
On its chain.

Maud
Seems to have the head of a fox,
The long ragged pelt of a giant fox hangs from her
shoulders, its brush and hind legs dangling below her
buttocks.
Its forepaws are knotted at her throat, its head is on her
head.

Felicity is crying with fear
As Maud spreads the blueish pale-fringed skin of a hind
over her shoulders
And knots its forelegs across her throat.
She fastens its mask on to the top of her head with a
hooked wire.
Felicity feels its hind legs tapping at the back of her
knees and calves.

She understands she has become a hind.
Her bowels coil and uncoil with fear.
She waits for whatever it is they are going to do to her.
She knows she has lost her way finally.
She catches and loses again the idea that Lumb will
somehow bring her out of all this.
She feels everything beginning to deepen again.
She forgets who she is or where she is.
The giant face of a rocking owl is ogling her
Over a pudgy unrecognisable body with swinging empty
sock breasts.
A giant expressionless badger with human arms and
fingers.
The smoke ropes them all together.
Lumb bobs under stag antlers, the russet bristly pelt of a
red stag flapping at his naked back.
Everything and everybody is moving
As if the music were the tumbling and boiling of a
cauldron.

Maud is leading Felicity on to the low rostrum.

145

She pushes Felicity's head down and forces her to kneel,
And then straddles her neck from behind and grips it
                                    between her thighs.
The music inside their bodies is doing what it wants at
                                    last
As if they were all somnambulist
They are no more awake than leaves in a whirlpool.

Maud sits lower, more heavily
Forcing Felicity's brows to the floorboards,
Gripping her by the hair.
The women are crying out in the hoarse pulse of the
                                    music.
Lumb mounts Felicity from behind, like a stag.

A giant hare-headed creature drops on human knees as if
                                    shot
And bows over folded human arms
In imitation of Felicity,
Shaking her head to the music, as if it were shaken.

In the shuttered room,
In the hot slowly-rending curtains of smoke,
Huge-headed woodland creatures from a nursery fairy tale
Are dropping on to their knees
Hugging their human bodies with human arms
As the music tears away the membranes, tearing them as
                                    the smoke tears,
And Lumb's mouth stretched open, like a painted mask,
Utters a long cry inside the cry
That is now torturing all of them
As they all cry together
As if they were being torn out of their bodies
And Maud's scream rips out the core of the sound
As she drags Felicity, by the hair,
Simultaneously forward and out
From between her knees.

146

Felicity
Tries to stand
As Maud, lifting both fists locked together above her head
Brings them down with all her crazy might on to
                                    Felicity's bowed nape.

Felicity's head flings back
As she sprawls forward two or three strides and collapses
                                    spreadeagled.
The hind's skin is plugged to the nape of her neck
Like a coat on a peg
By the hilt of Lumb's dagger
Whose blade is out of sight, inside her body.

Maud starts to speak.
The music prevents her, she speaks above the music
In a throat-gouging scream.
She is announcing
That this girl is not one of them
That she is his selected wife
That he is going to abandon them and run away with this
                                    girl
Like an ordinary man
With his ordinary wife.

The fuddled women grope for what has happened
And for what is being said
But their brains are still in the music
And nothing will separate.
They receive Maud's words as the revelation of
                                    everything.

Felicity's body lies still, no longer any part of what
                                    matters,
Twisted unhumanly, demonstrating her unimportance.

Lumb is kneeling.
He bows over her, close to her face,

His cheek almost touching her cheek
As he searches her face,
Hardly daring to breathe,
As if hardly daring to stir the air about her,
As if this were some horribly burned body
That has just dropped from a shocking height,
In which every nerve has been roasted
And every bone shattered, like a sackful of crockery.

With all his gentleness
He pulls on the hilt of the dagger,
As if gentleness intense enough
Could force a miracle
And unmake the black-mouthed slot
From which the frightening taper of steel
Continues to glide
Like a snake's endless length gliding from a hole.
The bright dove-crimson blood suddenly bulges out
                                           around it.

And all the time Maud is scourging his ear-nerves
With sounds that try only to mutilate.
The shock has sobered him, and stilled him,
Like a drastic injection.
His lips touch Felicity's cheek.
He sees her eyelashes clogged with tears,
He thinks this at least is a sign of life.
Then Maud's fingers hook down over his face,
She hauls his upper lips and nostrils upwards, as if she
                                  would tear his face off upwards.

Mrs Westlake
Slews Felicity's slack sack-heavy body
Away across the floor, by one ankle.
The attached pelt swirls after, in the dust.

Lumb tries to struggle free

But women have twisted to a weight like enfolding nets
                                        under water.
They are clinging to his knees, his waist, his arms, his neck
As if they too were drowning.

Maud has stripped the stag's pelt off him.
She is flogging him over his bald skull with the cable-
                          hard, twisted, horny stag's pizzle.
The women have made one undersea monster, heaving in
                                        throes.
Now he has wrenched his weapon from Maud.
He cuts a way out, flailing a path.
He fights to the stairway that leads up into the
                                        churchyard
And leaps up it and with great strides hurls out under the
                                        open,

And bounds twenty yards and stops.

Panting, he braces himself, forcing himself to look all
round, under control, assessing the world and the moment.
He looks back toward the church, still fighting clear of the
terror that grabbed him down there in the basement. No-
body is following.

The vast light of clouds and stilled evening sky, the
hardening, blue, cooling shapes of trees, are an enclosing
shock, as if he were hot metal plunged into water. Sweat
scalds the cross-hatching nail-wounds in his skin, the
lumping weals and claw-rips. He gulps recovery, looking
all round at the familiar land, intently, as if he had never
been here before, and would be away again in a few minutes.
Trembling, he starts to walk towards the gate into the
rectory garden.

His whole being is in fiery tatters.
He is whirling in blazing rags, like a blazing rag effigy
Cartwheeling down a mountain.

He grips the stag's pizzle.
He takes careful note of the tight-scrolled baby ferns on a
grave.
He clasps with his look
The all-suffering million-year gravel, which nothing can
hurt,
As if he could somehow anchor the holocaust of himself
Which seems to be hurtling through space, off some
brink,
Flinging out great streamers of flame and disintegrating.

With deliberate measure, like a drilled soldier, he moves
now to numbers.

In his bedroom he dresses
With a paced fury.
When one cuff-button resists him, he locks to it
With all his strength and attention
As to an antagonist,
While second after second splutters burning in the room,
like a fuse, and hot thoughts grab at him,
reflecting from every surface.

That somehow
Everything has to be cooled, everything has to be
dismantled,
Everybody back into their clothes and their discretion.

The explanation
For Felicity's body
Is a bomb
They will all have to dig out carefully somehow together.

Somehow everything
Will have to be cancelled, the whole error
Carefully taken apart
And the parts put back where they belonged.

Everybody has to return to exactly where they were,
To stillness, calm, and normality,
Everything has to be cleaned, groomed and made quiet,
                                        as at the start.

Suddenly he remembers Maud's voice, jarring his ear.
And he feels through all his muscles
The grip of Felicity's flesh on the dagger-blade as he
                                        pulled.
He sees, with electric shock fright in his every hair,
That horribly long blade still coming out and still coming
                                        out –

At the same moment
He sees through the window men in the churchyard.

The one glance
Flashbulbs all that has happened.

With hardly a footfall sound
Moving like a thought
He reaches his car and his fingers grip at the key which is
                                                        not there –

He ransacks every pocket reasoningly
With tightrope walker's care
While the evening thrushes ring out uncontrollably and
                                        the swifts flare past.

His memory jinks back through every chance
                                                misplacement.

He stands beside his car, stunned by the momentum of
                                                        time,
Like one wedged against the piling weight in mid-river at
                                        his limit of depth.

Then the men come round the house-end.

They have heard all that Maud can tell them.
Estridge is struggling with the irrelevance of trying to
                                                stay in control.
The murdered girl, the church basement full of naked,
    drugged wives, and ritualistic hocus pocus – all that is
    something for a full enquiry.
But his arguments are lost in mid-torrent.

Evans' trajectory is direct.
Garten's face is just a flag, for any prevailing gust.
Holroyd has been convinced and now intends to settle his
                                        private account publicly.
And a number of others
If there is to be any talking, intend to talk with boots
                                                        first.

Lumb comes towards them.
He is considering means of playing for a pause and
                          entangling everybody in words.
But Walsall's Alsatian
Already the most visibly incensed member of the mob
Liberated
Magnifies suddenly, bouncing towards Lumb
Like a hurtling, runaway wheel off a truck.
Lumb
Has a long second to marvel
At the demented personal malignity
Distorting the mask of this perfect stranger
As it hangs in mid-leap, level with his face, in a halo of
                          black bristles.

Then he is knocked backwards.
He lies, clear-headed, while the dog's jaws rave like a
                blurring power-saw within inches of his eyes.
He grips its muscled forelegs.
With all his might he wrenches them apart
And the dog's snarl splits to a damaged yell.

In one move Lumb is up and swinging the coal-sack body
                          through a full circle
Like a hammer-thrower
To fetch the dog's spine crack against the stone-built
                          corner of the garage.

The Alsatian collapses, gets up and careers away twisting
And collapses, chewing its yells.

The men pause, startled by his expert success.
But Walsall
Jerks a garden fork from the edge of a flower-bed and
                          lobs it like a harpoon.
It thumps Lumb's left shoulder, and hangs.
He tugs it out but his setback and the obvious wound are
                          two signals.

153

Nobody hears Estridge's restraining shouts about due
                                         process of law.

But Lumb
Has moved again, and has halted Evans
With a soil-solid flowerpot shattered against his chest,
And is away through the hedge.
He is running in the field above Smayle's garden.
He disappears.

Just as Westlake drives up behind the rectory and
                         scrambles out with his twelve bore.
The mob gallop after Lumb shouting varied strategies.
Westlake and Estridge huddle back into Westlake's car.

Easy and strong

And full out

With elbowing vigour to spare and confidence to spare

Lumb bounds away uphill.

He flings loose plans ahead of him,

Letting them settle over the whole region, shaping
themselves to the contours,

The woods, the roads, the paths and copses.

But looking back from that first skyline tree-fringe

He sees Garten and Holroyd and Evans are losing no
ground at all.

These men too are hardy animals of the same landscape

And their shouts rake him like missiles.

He lopes out along a hogback

Through ungrazed grass

Toughened with buttercup and young thistles

Toward a hill-crown clump of beeches, black against the
broad glare of sky,

Summit of power in the past.

Beyond that point, he knows, many escapes fall away
diversely into blue distance.

He hoists each stride, trying to be the earth and to toss
himself along weightlessly.

He shutters his awareness from the unmanageably tilting
planes of landscape to right and left

But a big thistle ahead is no help.

His fuel is burning too fast and smokily.

His knees tangle with their chemical limits.

His lungs are suddenly not those of a wolf or even a fox.

He imagines the furious micro-energy and stamina of the
blue-fly

But the idea takes no hold.

The miles of otherworld rootedness weigh in against him.

155

Static trees are a police of unmoving.
He flounders a little,
Seeming to crawl on the floor of his anxiety
Which is as wide and bare as the sucking space of the sky
                                    now poring over him,
And inspecting him tinily
Through a microscope,
Noticing most of all the immensity and immovability of
                                    the grass on all sides.

With jarring and clambering strides
He hauls himself up among the sheep-worn ramparts of
                                    roots
And under the twisted lichen-splotched, lichen-corroded
Torsos of the beeches
And the stirring leaf mass in its first tenderness.
In the draughty gap among trunks
He lets his stopped body, which he had forced to keep
                                    moving,
Loll and lean to a tree.
His lungs churn, his body flames,
He feels mangled
As if his blood had been pouring through rough iron
                                    channels.
He watches Garten and Evans, toiling on the near slope
                                    like plough-horses,
And far down to the right Holroyd running across.
He sees the whole vista scattered with jogging figures.

And now embracing the tree he flattens himself closely
                                    into it.
With fixed imagination he sinks nerves into the current of
                                    the powerline.
He gulps dense oxygen, recharging his trembling leg-
                                    muscles
Which already the strength no longer quite fits.
He feels his separateness, his healed-over smallness,
          among the loose stones and the hoof-printed dust.

156

These boles are bleak as ruins.
The leaf-towers are too lofty and sparse.
The empty sky looks in from every direction. He looks
                                        out at it,
And staring down into the too wide-open world he sees
                                        suddenly no hope.
The bronze polished light of the lowering sun is without
                                illusion of any sort.
It brings him a poisonous thinness like the taste of
                                        pennies.
Its shadows are prisonlike and depressing,
Hard-cut as machinery.
Every grass-blade wears its affliction of shadow.
The blueing bowl of landscape
Is a migraine of inescapable fixities, like sunglare in an
                                empty concrete pool.

A frightening sadness closes on him, as if he were
                                        shrinking,
And a futility
Grabs at his heart-beat, but he has already started
                                running away from it.

Holroyd's farm is below.
He vaults a wire, he runs downhill with long, jolting strides
Through a constellation of cows,
Statues of darkness in corollas of fire.
He registers aridity of corrugated iron, cruelty of old nails.
Stifling walls of tarred wood,
Creosote grubbiness of old sleepers walling a silage clamp,
The sterility of bare, stony hoof-hammered earth, fringed
                                with nettles and hemlock.

He climbs to the barn loft
Feeling like an early evening rat.
A minute's hiding, a minute's stolen relief
In the happy place, the nest among cornsacks
Where he can press his face into the fustiness.

157

His deep, scorching breaths suck in the lingering of her
                                                    perfume.

He groans under the collision of moments and sprawls,
                                                    like a casualty,
And with new fervour clenches his hands,
Opening all his loosened fibres to the globe's power
And releasing a flood of sweat.
He makes himself nothing, he empties his body of all its
                                                    history,
For the inrush of renewals and instructions.

He almost sleeps, in a luxury
Of these shortening seconds
In which they cannot possibly touch him
Before those seconds arrive made of their feet, their
                                                    shouts, their eyes.

For a long fantasy he is lost
In details of a court defence
But suddenly shouts are stabbing everywhere around him,
                                                    like torchbeams.

He shrinks.
He sheds everything into hungry darkness, he yields into
                                                    a raw black fieriness.
He launches his whole being into whatever it is that is
                                                    waiting for him.

An impulse bends him, with alacrity and lightness,
At the cock-loft window
As voices and steps climb the ladder to the loft behind
                                                    him.

He drops twelve feet
Crosses through the near-empty dutch barn,
And runs out across grass, under a halo of gnats.
And now every stride
Multiplies towards freedom.

And every second
Deepens the defences behind him.
A hare jumps out of the earth and scuds away ahead,
                                   ears up, leaning like a yacht,
Like a guide.

Then shouts catch and trip him, eyes have gripped him.
A landrover is bounding over turf, hands cling where they
                                                         can.
Runners are bobbing, heels drive deep moons among the
                                               wolf-spiders.

A banked thorn hedge, a tatter wool gap, is behind him.
Barbed wire, padded with bullock's hair, is beneath him.
A high rail is strong enough, he vaults over it.
Sheep pour this way and that.
Bullocks gallop off their shock of excitement,
While the air rips in his throat, like a dry piston,
And the blood crisps on his left hand
And all the time his shoulder
Gnaws as if the whole arm-load
Were a swinging iron trap.

Till he topples over the rusty rail
Into the young plantation which is Hagen's boundary.

He looks back
Just in time to see the landrover misjudge a banked hedge
And keel over, flinging out figures.
Small cries come to him.
He does not stay to identify
Dunworth sitting with his head in his hands letting blood
                                        drip into the grass,
Or Walsall twisted at the awkward angle
Of minimum pain, eyes closed from the pursuit,
Or Evans and Garten
Leading with pitchforks away from the capsized vehicle.

Lumb splashes through brambles among the sparse young
                                                    conifers.
Well into the thick, he drops, panting and listening.
Now he concentrates each particular second, cramming it
                                            with recovery.
Long horizontal rays
Finger through the wood, kindling the floss-winged
                                                ephemera.
Safely distant pheasants challenge.
He closes his eyes, trying to feel back to the sure root of
                                                    guidance.
He feels his sinewy second wind clearing itself, and his
                                            blood renewing.
He pushes on, foxy-cautious and alert
In a fierce haste, that lifts aside the brambles delicately
                                        as setting a snare.
The low spare plantation is crisp and weary in the late sun.
A few butterflies hither and thither together aimlessly.
Specks with legs crawl glittering on stems, as if in a
                                                dusty sweat.
Wherever he looks down
Through the rafters of grass and weeds
Ants are racing from crisis to crisis.

Baffled shouts probe the plantation.
He flattens under brambles, in a drainage channel,
And watches Garten wading past, face glossed in the level
                                                        sun,
The pitchfork glinting.

As the shouts go off
He sidles along low and comes to a rail and peers over
To reconnoitre forward.
He pulls himself erect.
A light electric shock touches him.
The landrover's horribly familiar mass is there, ten yards
                                                        away.

It emits a shout.
160

Lumb realises with nausea he has come in a circle, like a
                                          simple fool.
Simultaneously
An explosion encloses his head, like a sudden bag.
Shot slashes weak leaves.
A pain clubs his fingertip.

He drops, dragging backwards, and turns, and runs
In lit smoking of pollen and dust.
Another blind shot wounds the wood's depth dully.
He leaps on different grounds.

And now in a roofless tumblestone linney, he props
                                    himself back in a corner.
Burdock, nettles, brambles mound over tile-heaps and
                                          jags of beams.
He fights to quiet his breath forcibly and to repair his
                                          shaking body.
The sweat melts on his face full in the facing hot-coin sun.

A crackling approaches, Lumb withers into his corner,
And Evans, pushing in over the debris, positions himself
                                          leisurely
And urinates ponderously on to a camp of nettles, with a
                                          hard sigh.

Turning, contemplative, he meets Lumb's stare
Who even now feels he might slide aside from under this
                                    confrontation unseen.
But Evans' incredulous 'Bloody Hell!' splits with a bellow
                                    to the whole landscape.
The gloating pitchfork, prongs downfanged, inches
                                    gleaming toward Lumb
Slowly tightening this corner to certainty
While Evans' face tightens, as if he were to splinter the
                                    levelled shaft in his grip.

Lumb leaps suddenly

Cat-scrambling upwards, up the rotten stonework
Which crumbles scattering over him.
But he scrambles higher,
Abandons to the expected blow
That part of his body which must protect the rest.
Sure enough, a sickening weight has snagged him
Above the hip, but he drags on upwards,
Lifting the weight with him
And half-turns, and half-sitting on the wall top
Grips the crutch of the sun-gleaming tine
And eases his body off the parallel hidden one.

Evans, cursing, levering, is trying to fork Lumb off the
                                        wall-top like a bale,
And he sees too late
The stone block spinning in air in a shower of dust.
For a black vital second he loses contact with everything.
Surprised he finds himself numbed and criss-cross
                        struggling to get up from the rubble
With an ugly taste in his mouth, and a detached
                                    precarious feeling,
While slowly understanding swarms back to centre.
His alarm to the wood is a disgorging beast-roar clotted
                                        with obscenities,
A rage as infinite as it is helpless.
But Lumb has vanished.

Evans strays out of the linney, dizzied and wanting to sit
                                                down.
His face wears a thick mask of drained woodenness,
                            which he dare not touch.

But Lumb
Beyond caution is bounding
Through undergrowth, crashing like a hurt stag
That feels itself surrounded.
He vaults a rail and gallops out on to parkland and into a
                                great spaciousness.

And keeps on running.
And sees Hagen's squat elegant residence swinging into
view on the right.

All the anchored bulls recoil, as if interconnected,
Then focus
Under their neck-humps.

He runs with freed limbs.
He bounds down the new-grassed slope toward the long
flat of the lake,
Gold-hot and molten, under the late sky.
And toward the skyline beyond, and the tree-lumped
frieze which is the highway.

He runs imagining
Mountains of golden spirit, he springs across their crests.
He has plugged his energy appeal into the inexhaustible
earth.
He rides in the air behind his shoulders with a whip of
hard will
Like a charioteer.
He imagines he is effortless Adam, before weariness
entered, leaping for God.

He safeguards the stroke of his heart
From the wrenching of ideas.
He hoards his wasteful mind like a last mouthful.

He runs
In a balancing stillness
Like a working gleam on the nape of a waterfall,
And he is exulting
That the powers have come back they truly have come
back
They have not abandoned him.

At the same time

He runs badly hurt, his blood inadequate,
Hurling his limbs anyhow
Lumpen and leaden, and there is no more air.

His whole body is an orgasm of burning, a seized-up
                                        engine.
His mouth hangs open, forgotten as in an accident.
His face has become a mere surface, like his thorn-ripped
                                        shins

And he knows
He has lost every last help
Of the grass and the trees,
He knows that the sky no longer ushers towards him
                    glowing hieroglyphs of endowment,
That he is now ordinary, and susceptible
To extinction,
That his precious and only body
Is nothing more than some radio-transmitter, a standard
                                        structure,
Tipped from an empty dinghy by a wave
In the middle of a sea grey and nameless.

And he knows that the puncture in his side
Which will be so round and tiny
If ever he comes to look at it
Is black with deepness, blue-black, like the crater of a
                                        drawn tooth
But unthinkably deeper, and more real
Than anything on this earth, anything containable by
                                        this sky.

And he sees
Over the jouncing tops of his stride
Through his jarred and spilling retina
The car
Gliding down the avenue of chestnuts
To reach the lakeside before him.

But he does not feel
The pressure
And ten magnifications
Of Hagen's telescope, in which he now jigs like a puppet.

As the sun touches the skyline, under the red-plumed sky
Lumb reaches the lake's edge.
The quilted parkland behind him is aswarm with running
                                        men and shouts.
Westlake and Estridge have left the car.
They are coming along the lake's edge.
Westlake is carrying his gun.

Lumb understands quite clearly at last
Why he has been abandoned to these crying beings
Who are all hurrying towards him
In order to convert him to mud from which plants grow
                                and which cattle tread.
He sees the reeds sticking up out of the water
So conceitedly dull in their rootedness
Like books in a technical library.
He sees the lakewater
Simply waste liquid flowed in here, and collected by
                                                inertia,
From the gutters of space
Where it is worthless and accidental –
A spiritless by-product
Of the fact that things exist at all.
He knows now that this land
This embroidery of stems and machinery of cells
Is an ignorance, waiting in a darkness –
He knows at last why it has become so.

But he does not step to the end of this overhanging
                                                thought.
He collects himself, and concentrates
On the small target, the small carefulness
Of liberating himself

From this crux of moments and shouts and water-margin
With his bones whole and warm, his nerves intact,
In his own bag of skin.
He sees Estridge has stopped, and is sitting, holding his
                                                    chest.
He sees Westlake stumbling closer.

He enters
The crackling of reeds, the silken complexities of the mud,
The bubbling belly-gas of the roots.
He wades into coldness, with plunges and flounderings,
                                                    deepening,
Eager to sink himself
Equal to the wildness and finality of the cold grip.

A waterhen
Ploughs a spattering runway from beside him and out
    across the clear reaches of midlake depth and subsides
    with a soft crash into the reedbank opposite.
Lumb looks down at the freckled brown earthenware of
                        the family of eggs, on the clump of decay.
In that moment's pause, Westlake's shot
Smokes a boiling track through the reeds towards him
                                                    and beyond him.
Lumb's unhurt arm jumps to protect his face
And the long carpet of echoes unrolls
Across the still land into the upholstered distance.

Lumb presses deeper, leaning into the surface blade of the
                                                    water,
And Westlake fires again. Lumb's head and shoulders
Gesticulate in the smoking pattern.
He pushes out further, chesting the cold press, till he
                                                    pauses
In the oily fringe of lilies.
His broad ripples go riding out over the clear depth
                                                    beyond
Which is floored with a pale jungle.

And he sees
The box-profile of a truck nudging up the tree-rough
                                                    skyline
Against the cooling sky.
He hears it change gear.
He hears around it the whole cooling world, hung like a
                                                    glass bell,
Simmering with evening birds.

He balances,
Narrowing himself to pierce a disappearance, to become
                                                    infinitesimal
To slip through the crack of this place
With its clutching and raging people, its treacherous
                                        lanes, its rooted houses.

Hagen, leaning in the window-frame,
Cheekbone snug to the glossed walnut, introduces his first
        love to the panorama of his marriage and retirement.
The Mannlicher ·318
Regards Lumb's distant skull dutifully, with perfectly
                                tooled and adjusted concentration.
Germanic precision, slender goddess
Of Hagen's devotions
And the unfailing bride
Of his ecstasies in the primal paradise, and the midwife of
                                                    Eden's beasts,
Painlessly delivered, with a little blood,
And laid at his feet
As if fresh from the Creator's furnace, as if to be named.
With her, only with her
Hagen feels his life stir on its root.

The crossed hairs have settled on Lumb's crown.
And now the trigger
Caresses in oil, and the kiss of sweetness jolts softly
                                        through Hagen's bones.

The burned muzzle flings back.
The crack
Shattering a globe, drives its deep spike.
And the whole scene splits open under the long slash, like
                                        a stomach.

Lumb
Poised for his swimming plunge
Smacks face-down
Hard, like a flat hand on to the water.

The hunchbacked bullet has already escaped among
                                        lily-roots.

Lumb floats, splayed like a stunned frog, face downwards.
Every visible figure is frozen, a parkful of statues.
Slowly the tangled dark lump among the lily pads starts
                                        to churn
As if trying to flee in every direction simultaneously.

It flails the lake's sky-colours, heaving out slow wings of
                                cold evening shadow.

They have dragged him out
Onto the bank
As the strewn western clouds smudge ashen.
The blood from his burst head washes his face and neck
In thin solution and ropy lumps,
And puddles black the hoofprints under his head.
Lily stems cling to him.
His pursuers stand in a ring
Like sightseers around the maneater's long body.
The bulls have come up in a wider wondering circle,
    tossing sniffs towards the odour and the frightening
    object.

Lumb is carried back
Strung under a fence-rail
168

Through the darkening countryside.

In the graveyard
A group of women
Like people standing around for no reason still
                                    magnetised after an accident
Are waiting near Felicity's body
Which lies under a curtain, in the church porch.

The men carry Lumb down into the basement.
Maud is sitting alone there in the dark, as if now totally
                                       imbecile.
They switch on lights.
Maud watches
As they pile chairs, tables, the goggling masks and the
                                   jumble-sale of skins,
Everything combustible, in the middle of the room, over
                                   the bloodstain.
They lay out Lumb on top of the pile, on a table.

Felicity
Has to be part of a presentable accident.
They take her body forcibly from Garten
And bring it into the basement, where they find Maud
Curled on the floor around Lumb's dagger, her temple to
                         the boards, as if quite comfortable in death,
And like a foetus asleep, with crossed ankles.
They stretch her out on one side of Lumb.
They leave Lumb's dagger in position because nobody
                                 wants to touch it.
They lay Felicity on the other side of Lumb.
So the three lie, faces upward, with touching hands, on
                                 the narrow table,
On top of the pyre.
Lumb's eyes are closed, but the women's eyes are wide.
The men arrange all this in deep silence, entranced by the
                                 deep satisfaction of it.

Evans brings a can of petrol.
Holroyd anoints the pile, he douches the three bodies.

Windows are smashed out for vents.

Holroyd spatters a petrol fuse up the stair and out into
                                        the churchyard,
Then drops a match on to it.

All evidence goes up.

EPILOGUE

EPILOGUE

In a straggly sparse village on the West Coast of Ireland, on a morning in May – a morning of gust and dazzle – three small girls came to the priest where he sat in his study gazing at an open page of St Ignatius.

They brought something wrapped in a black waterproof folder. A stranger, a man, who had gone off in a car, had left it on a boulder down by the sea-lough. The priest unwrapped the folder and discovered a tattered notebook. Looking closely at the densely corrected pages he saw it was full of verse. He became curious about the man. He asked the girls more.

They had been playing among the rocks, and there wasn't a soul to be seen. Then they got a fright. One minute there was just rocks, and the next minute there was this man, right beside them, sitting on a rock, watching them.

Before they could run off, he spoke. He asked them the name of the lough. Then he wanted to know the name of that mountain across the lough. Then of that other mountain, and the mountain beyond it. So with all the mountains in sight, mountain beyond mountain, far away to North and to South, the girls had to name them or say they didn't know. Finally the man asked them if they'd ever seen a miracle. They had not.

He made them sit down on the rocks beside him. They promised that whatever happened they would not move or speak or make the slightest sound. Then he put the back of his hand to his mouth. He pursed his lips against the back of his hand. The girls waited. Suddenly their nerves seemed to shrivel, like a hair held in fire. An uncanny noise was coming from the back of the man's hand. A peculiar, warbling thin sound. It was like a tiny gentle screaming. A wavering, wringing, awful sound, that caught hold of their

173

heads and was nearly painful. It was like a fine bloody thread being pulled through their hearts.

The man stared at the lough and the sound went out over the water. On and on and on. And the girls sat, petrified, staring at the man. He was solemn-looking, long-faced, dark-faced, and his bald shiny head was lumped with scars.

He stopped his noise abruptly. The silence was even worse. The girls looked where he was looking. Something was standing up out of the water at the lough's edge. It was a beast of some kind, gazing towards them.

Now the noise started again, but this time much more softly. The girls could feel it plucking at different places inside them. It made them want to cry. And the beast came up out of the water.

It was like nothing the girls had ever seen, unless it was like a big weasel. It came up the gravelly beach below the rocks with that merry, hump-backed, snake-headed gallop of weasels. It came on over the rocks. It disappeared and they thought it had gone. It reappeared much closer and bigger. And all the time the man kept on with his strange, soft, painful cry.

Till at last the creature was sitting there in front of them, the size of a big cat, its dark fur all clawed with wet, craning towards the man, sniffing and shivering, so he could have reached out his hand and touched it, and the girls could smell the wild smell of the fish of the lough.

Again the man was silent. He sat watching the beast. And the beast went on trembling and sniffing and craning towards him. It seemed to be getting ready to jump into his lap. One of the girls could stand it no longer. She jerked in her foot, and hunched herself tighter, and a whimper escaped her.

The beast stood erect and stared. It stood up on its hind legs, like a person, and stared at them, quite still, as if they were very far away. The girls saw its foreign eyes, its wide whiskers. They thought they were going to be attacked at last, and got ready to shriek. Instead, it turned away and dropped off the back of its rock, and went on down over

174

the rocks and over the beach and into the water. And all the time the man sat watching it without a word. The creature stood up again, in the shallow water, looking back. Then it had gone.

The priest listened to this story, and smiled at the excitement of the three girls.

'If that is a miracle,' he said finally, 'To bring an otter up out of the lough, then what must that poor man think of the great world itself, this giant, shining beauty that God whistled up out of the waters of chaos?'

And as he spoke the priest was suddenly carried away by his words. His thoughts flew up into a great fiery space, and who knows what spark had jumped on to him from the flushed faces of the three girls? He seemed to be flying into an endless, blazing sunrise, and he described the first coming of Creation, as it rose from the abyss, an infinite creature of miracles, made of miracles and teeming miracles. And he went on, describing this creature, giving it more and more dazzlingly-shining eyes, and more and more glorious limbs, and heaping it with greater and more extraordinary beauties, till his heart was pounding and he was pacing the room talking about God himself, and the tears pouring from his eyes fell shattering and glittering down the front of his cassock.

The girls became dull, and the moment his words paused they vanished through the doorway. The priest hardly noticed, he was so astonished by his own emotion. He sat down, trembling and faint, as in a fever. He thought something supernatural had happened. Then he saw the notebook again, lying on the table, and he remembered the otter and the strange way it had come up out of the lough because a man whistled. He opened the notebook and began to decipher the words. He found a pen and clean paper and began to copy out the verses.

What will you make of half a man
Half a face
A ripped edge

His one-eyed waking
Is the shorn sleep of aftermath

His vigour
The bone-deformity of consequences

His talents
The deprivations of escape

How will you correct
The veteran of negatives
And the survivor of cease?

I hear your congregations at their rapture

Cries from birds, long ago perfect
And from the awkward gullets of beasts
That will not chill into syntax.

And I hear speech, the bossed Neanderthal brow-ridge
Gone into beetling talk
The Java Man's bone grinders sublimed into chat.

Words buckle the voice in tighter, closer
Under the midriff
Till the cry rots, and speech

Is a fistula

Eking and deferring
Like a stupid or a crafty doctor
With his year after year

Of sanguinary nostrums
Of almosts and their tomorrows

Through a lifetime of fees.

Who are you?

The spider clamps the bluefly – whose death panic
Becomes sudden soulful absorption.

A stoat throbs at the nape of the lumped rabbit
Who watches the skylines fixedly.

Photographs of people – open-mouthed
In the gust of being shot and falling

And you grab me
So the blood jumps into my teeth

And 'Quick!' you whisper, 'O quick!'
And 'Now! Now! Now!'

Now what?

That I hear the age of the earth?

That I feel
My mother lift me up from between her legs?

At the top of my soul
A box of dolls.

In the middle of my soul
A circus of gods.

At the bottom of my soul
The usual mess of squabblers.

In front of me
A useful-looking world, a thrilling weapon.

Behind me
A cave

Inside the cave, some female groaning
In labour –

Or in hunger –

Or in fear, or sick, or forsaken –

Or –

At this point, I feel the sun's strength.
I take a few still-aimless happy steps.

The lark sizzles in my ear
Like a fuse –

A prickling fever
A flush of the swelling earth –

When you touch his grains, who shall stay?

Over the lark's crested tongue
Under the lark's crested head
A prophecy

From the core of the blue peace

178

From the sapphire's flaw

From the sun's blinding dust

I watched a wise beetle
Walking about inside my body

I saw a tree
Grow inward from my navel

Hawks clashed their courtship
Between my ears.

Slowly I filled up with the whole world.
Only one thing stayed outside me, in the glare.

You beckoned.

In a world where all is temporary
And must pass for its opposite

The trousseau of the apple
Came by violence into my possession.

I neglected to come to degree of nature
In the patience of things.

I forestalled God —

I assailed his daughter.

Now I lie at the road's edge.
People come and go.

Dogs watch me.

Collision with the earth has finally come –
How far can I fall?

A kelp, adrift
In my feeding substance

A mountain
Rooted in stone of heaven

A sea
Full of moon-ghost, with mangling waters

Dust on my head
Helpless to fit the pieces of water
A needle of many Norths

Ark of blood
Which is the magic baggage old men open
And find useless, at the great moment of need

Error on error
Perfumed
With a ribbon of fury

Trying to be a leaf
In your kingdom
For a moment I am a leaf
And your fulness comes

And I reel back
Into my face and hands

Like the electrocuted man
Banged from his burst straps

180

I heard the screech, sudden –
Its steel was right inside my skull
It scraped all round, inside it
Like the abortionist's knife.

My blood lashed and writhed on its knot –
Its skin is so thin, and so blind,
And earth is so huge, so hard, wild
And so nearly nothing
And so final with its gravity stone –

My legs, though, were already galloping to help
The woman who wore a split lopsided mask –

That was how the comedy began.

Before I got to her – it was ended
And the curtain came down.

But now, suddenly,
Again the curtain goes up.

This is no longer the play.

The mask is off.

Once I said lightly
Even if the worst happens
We can't fall off the earth.

And again I said
No matter what fire cooks us
We shall be still in the pan together.

And words twice as stupid.
Truly hell heard me.

She fell into the earth
And I was devoured.

Music, that eats people
That transfixes them
On its thorns, like a shrike
To cut up at leisure

Or licks them all over carefully gently
Like a tiger
Before leaving nothing but the hair of the head
And the soles of the feet

Is the maneater
On your leash.

But all it finds of me, when it picks me up

Is what you have
Already
Emptied and rejected.

The rain comes again
A tightening, a prickling in
On the soft-rotten gatepost.

But the stars
Are sunbathing
On the shores
Of the sea whose waves

Pile in from your approach
182

An unearthly woman wading shorewards
With me in your arms

The grey in my hair.

This is the maneater's skull.
These brows were the Arc de Triomphe
To the gullet.

The deaf adder of appetite
Coiled under. It spied through these nacelles
Ignorant of death.

And the whole assemblage flowed hungering through the
long ways.
Its cry
Quieted the valleys.

It was looking for me.

I was looking for you.

You were looking for me.

I see the oak's bride in the oak's grasp.

Nuptials among prehistoric insects
The tremulous convulsion
The inching hydra strength
Among frilled lizards

Dropping twigs, and acorns, and leaves.

183

The oak is in bliss
Its roots
Lift arms that are a supplication
Crippled with stigmata
Like the sea-carved cliffs earth lifts
Loaded with dumb, uttering effigies
The oak seems to die and to be dead
In its love-act.

As I lie under it

In a brown leaf nostalgia

An acorn stupor

A perilously frail safety.

She rides the earth
On an ass, on a lion.
She rides the heavens
On a great white bull.

She is an apple.
Whoever plucks her
Nails his heart
To the leafless tree.

The huntsmen, on top of their swaying horse-towers,
Faces raw as butcher's blocks, are angry.
They have lost their fox.

They have lost most of their hounds.

184

I can't help.

The one I hunt
The one
I shall rend to pieces

Whose blood I shall dab on your cheek

Is under my coat.

❖

A primrose petal's edge
Cuts the vision like laser.

And the eye of a hare
Strips the interrogator naked
Of all but some skin of terror –
A starry frost.

Who is this?
She reveals herself, and is veiled.
Somebody

Something grips by the nape
And bangs the brow, as against a wall
Against the untouchable veils

Of the hole which is bottomless

Till blood drips from the mouth.

❖

Waving goodbye, from your banked hospital bed,
Waving, weeping, smiling, flushed

It happened
You knocked the world off, like a flower-vase.

It was the third time. And it smashed.

I turned
I bowed
In the morgue I kissed
Your temple's refrigerated glazed
As rained-on graveyard marble, my
Lips queasy, heart non-existent

And straightened
Into sun-darkness

Like a pillar over Athens

Defunct

In the glaring metropolis of cameras.

I said goodbye to earth
I stepped into the wind
Which entered the tunnel of fire
Beneath the mountain of water

I arrived at light
Where I was shadowless
I saw the snowflake crucified
Upon the nails of nothing

I heard the atoms praying
To enter his kingdom
To be broken like bread
On a dark sill, and to bleed.

The swallow – rebuilding –
Collects the lot
From the sow's wallow.

But what I did only shifted the dust about.
And what crossed my mind
Crossed into outer space.

And for all rumours of me read obituary.
What there truly remains of me
Is that very thing – my absence.

So how will you gather me?

I saw my keeper
Sitting in the sun –

If you can catch that, you are the falcon of falcons.

The night wind, muscled with rain,
Is going to tug out
The trees like corks –

Just as in the dream –
A voice quaking lit heaven
The stone tower flies.

A night
To scamper naked
To the dry den

Where one who would have devoured me is driven off

By a wolf.

The viper fell from the sun
Jerked and lay in the road's dust,
Started horribly to move, as I watched it.

A radiant goose dropped from a fire-quake heaven,
Slammed on to earth beside me
So hard, it bounced me off my feet.

Something dazzling crashed on the hill field,
Elk-antlered, golden-limbed, a glowing mass
That started to get up.

I stirred, like a discarded foetus,
Already grey-haired,
In a blowing of bright particles.

A hand out of a hot cloud
Held me its thumb to suck.

Lifted me to the dug that grew
Out of the brow of a lioness.

A doctor extracted
From my blood its tusk

Excavated
The mountain-root from my body

Excised
The seven-seas' spring from under my eye-tooth

Emptied my skull
Of clouds and stars

Pounded up what was left
Dried it and lit it and read by its flame
A story to his child

188

About a God
Who ripped his mother's womb
And entered it, with a sword and a torch

To find a father.

The coffin, spurred by its screws,
Took a wrong turning.

The earth can't balance its load
Even to start.

The creaking heavens
Will never get there.

As for me
All I have

For an axle

Is your needle
Through my brains.

The grass-blade is not without
The loyalty that never was beheld.

And the blackbird
Sleeking from common anything and worm-dirt
Balances a precarious banner
Gold on black, terror and exultation.

The grim badger with armorial mask
Biting spade-steel, teeth and jaw-strake shattered,

Draws that final shuddering battle cry
Out of its backbone.

Me too,
Let me be one of your warriors.

Let your home
Be my home. Your people
My people.

Churches topple
Like the temples before them.

The reverberations of worship
Seem to help
Collapse such erections.

In all that time
The river
Has deepened its defile
Has been its own purification

Between your breasts

Between your thighs

I know well
You are not infallible

I know how your huge your unmanageable
Mass of bronze hair shrank to a twist
190

As thin as a silk scarf, on your skull,
And how your pony's eye darkened larger

Holding too lucidly the deep glimpse
After the humane killer

And I had to lift your hand for you

While your chin sank to your chest
With the sheer weariness
Of taking away from everybody
Your envied beauty, your much-desired beauty

Your hardly-used beauty

Of lifting away yourself
From yourself

And weeping with the ache of the effort

The sun, like a cold kiss in the street –
A mere disc token of you.

Moon – a smear
Of your salivas, cold, cooling.

Bite. Again, bite.

Sometimes it comes, a gloomy flap of lightning,
Like the flushed gossip
With the tale that kills

Sometimes it strengthens very slowly
What is already here –
A tree darkening the house.

The saviour
From these veils of wrinkle and shawls of ache

Like the sun
Which is itself cloudless and leafless

Was always here, is always as she was.

Having first given away pleasure –
Which is hard –
What is there left to give?
There is pain.

Pain is hardest of all.
It cannot really be given.

It can only be paid down
Equal, exactly,
To what can be no part of falsehood.

This payment is that purchase.

Looking for her form
I find only a fern.

Where she should be waiting in the flesh
Stands a sycamore with weeping letters.

I have a memorial too.

Where I lay in space
Is the print of the earth which trampled me

Like a bunch of grapes.

Now I am being drunk
By a singing drunkard.

A man hangs on
To a bare handful of hair.

A woman hangs on
To a bare handful of flesh.

Who is it
Reaches both hands into the drop

Letting flesh and hair
Follow if they can?

When the still-soft eyelid sank again
Over the stare
Still bright as if alive

The chiselled threshold
Without a murmur
Ground the soul's kernel

Till blood welled.

And your granite –
Anointed –
Woke.

Stirred.

The sea grieves all night long.
The wall is past groaning.
The field has given up –
It can't care any more.

Even the tree
Waits like an old man
Who has seen his whole family murdered.

Horrible world

Where I let in again –
As if for the first time –
The untouched joy.

Hearing your moan echo, I chill. I shiver.

I know
You can't stay with those trees.

I know
The river is only fabled to be orphan.

I know
The flowers also look for you, and die looking.

194

Just as the sun returns every day
As if owned.

Like me
These are neither your brides, nor your grooms.

Each of us is nothing
But the fleeting warm pressure

Of your footfall

As you pace
Your cage of freedom.

Faces lift out of the earth
Moistly-lidded, and gazing unfocussed
Like babies new born.

And with cries like the half-cry
Of a near-fatally wounded person
Not yet fallen, but already unconscious.

And these are the ones
Who are trying to tell
Your name.

From age to age
Nothing bequeathed
But a gagged yell

A clutchful of sod

And libraries
Of convalescence.

I skin the skin
Take the eye from the eye
Extract the entrails from the entrails

I scrape the flesh from the flesh
Pluck the heart
From the heart
Drain away the blood from the blood

Boil the bones till nothing is left
But the bones

I pour away the sludge of brains
Leaving simply the brains

Soak it all
In the crushed-out oil of the life

Eat

Eat

What steel was it the river poured
Horizontally
Into the sky's evening throat –

Put out the sun.

The steel man, in his fluttering purples,
Is lifted from the mould's fragments.

I breathe on him

Terrors race over his skin.

He almost lives

Who dare meet you.

Calves harshly parted from their mamas
Stumble through all the hedges in the country
Hither thither crying day and night
Till their throats will only grunt and whistle.

After some days, a stupor sadness
Collects them again in their field.
They will never stray any more.
From now on, they only want each other.

So much for calves.
As for the tiger
He lies still
Like left luggage

He is roaming the earth light, unseen.

He is safe.

Heaven and hell have both adopted him.

A bang – a burning –
I opened my eyes
In a vale crumbling with echoes.

A solitary dove
Cries in the tree – I cannot bear it.

From this centre
It wearies the compass.

Am I killed?
Or am I searching?

Is this the rainbow silking my body?

Which wings are these?

The dead man lies, marching here and there
In the battle for life, without moving.

He prays he will escape for what comes after.
At least that he'll escape. So he lies still.

But it arrives
Invisible as a bullet
And the dead man flings up his arms
With a cry
Incomprehensible in every language

And from that moment
He never stops trying to dance, trying to sing
And maybe he dances and sings

Because you kissed him.

If you miss him, he stays dead
Among the inescapable facts.

Every day the world gets simply
Bigger and bigger

198

And smaller and smaller

Every day the world gets more
And more beautiful

And uglier and uglier.

Your comings get closer.
Your goings get worse.

Your tree – your oak
A glare

Of black upward lightning, a wriggling grab
Momentary
Under the crumbling of stars.

A guard, a dancer
At the pure well of leaf.

Agony in the garden. Annunciation
Of clay, water and the sunlight.
They thunder under its roof.
Its agony is its temple.

Waist-deep, the black oak is dancing
And my eyes pause
On the centuries of its instant
As gnats
Try to winter in its wrinkles.

The seas are thirsting
Towards the oak.

The oak is flying
Astride the earth.

199

Glare out of just crumpled grass –
Blinded, I blink.

Glare out of muddled clouds –
I go in.

Glare out of house-gloom –
I close my eyes.

And the darkness too is aflame.

So you have come and gone again
With my skin.